PHENOMENOLOGY OF THE ALIEN

Northwestern University
Studies in Phenomenology
and
Existential Philosophy

Founding Editor †James M. Edie

General Editor Anthony J. Steinbock

Associate Editor John McCumber

PHENOMENOLOGY OF THE ALIEN

Basic Concepts

Bernhard Waldenfels

Translated from the German by
Alexander Kozin and Tanja Stähler

Northwestern University Press
Evanston, Illinois

Northwestern University Press
www.nupress.northwestern.edu

Translation funded by Volkswagen Stiftung.

Printed in the United States of America

10 9 8 7 6 5 4 3 2 1

Library of Congress Cataloging-in-Publication Data

Waldenfels, Bernhard, 1934–
    [Grundmotive einer Phänomenologie des Fremden. English]
    Phenomenology of the alien : basic concepts / Bernhard Waldenfels ; translated from the German by Alexander Kozin and Tanja Stähler.
        p. cm. — (Northwestern University studies in phenomenology and existential philosophy)
    Includes bibliographical references.
    ISBN 978-0-8101-2756-2 (cloth : alk. paper) — ISBN 978-0-8101-2757-9 (pbk. : alk. paper)
    1. Other (Philosophy) 2. Phenomenology. I. Title. II. Series: Northwestern University studies in phenomenology & existential philosophy.
BD460.O74W3413 2011
121.2—dc22

                                                                            2011009404

♾ The paper used in this publication meets the minimum requirements of the American National Standard for Information Sciences—Permanence of Paper for Printed Library Materials, ANSI Z39.48-1992.

Contents

PHENOMENOLOGY OF THE ALIEN

Introduction

Facets of the Alien

To pose the alien as a special theme is to have missed it already. For it means to begin from the place of the familiar and the known, and if the journey goes as planned, to expect to return to the same place. Most certainly, the experience of the alien will bring about a change, maybe even a catharsis. Yet, in the end, the original familiarity will prevail; it might even expand or deepen itself. And since the alien is not harmless, it might alienate us from ourselves. Hence the perpetual motivation to resist, avoid, or assimilate the alien. However, giving in to this motivation is to make the subject remain at home with himself or herself. It also means that the strong fortifications of an order which excludes the unordered should remain in place, preventing the alien from disturbing us from within. The alien can inspire curiosity and imagination, it can even enlighten us about ourselves—all this must be granted. Yet as soon as the alien breaks into the arcanum of freedom and reason, it trips the "chaos" alarm. Freedom and reason take up their arms. They fight because otherwise they would need to give up on themselves. But, inevitably, alienness leads to hostility, which only escalates, with each involved party becoming more and more committed to their belief that they alone have right on their side. We become watchful of the other, moving closer together. There are certain safety devices built into an experiential network, which originates in what is one's own and seeks a hold in what is common. Assumed to be coming from the outside, the alien is expected to carry its identification at all times as if it were an intruder. It then becomes subjected to evaluation and judgment. As a result, an everyday moral, political, religious, cultural, and also intellectual quarantine is imposed on it.

If we take the alien, in contrast, as something that cannot be pinned down, if we take it as something which seeks us out in our own home (German *heimsuchen*) by disturbing, enticing, or terrifying us, by surpassing our expectations and eluding our grasp, then this means that the experience of *the* alien always affects our own experience and thus turns into a *becoming-alien of experience*. Alienness is self-referential, and it is contagious. Its effects precede any thematization. A phenomenology of the alien, which was already anticipated by Husserl in several of his groundbreaking concepts (namely, alien experience, alien ego, alien body, or alien world), has the makings of a science that approaches the alien in toto, taking the radicality of alien experience seriously rather than resting content with the reductions to such problems as constitution, understanding, or the practical recognition of the alien. Many familiar problems acquire new contours when the shadow of the alien falls on them. A phenomenologist who confronts the demands of a xenology will find herself in the company of those who allow themselves to be inspired by Marcel Mauss, Georg Simmel, Walter Benjamin, Ludwig Wittgenstein, or Mikhail Bakhtin—not to mention congenial literary figures like Kafka, Musil, Celan, Valéry, and Calvino. However, the world of the arts lives by a different calendar. The artistic *sensorium* could easily surpass the limits of self-certainty and *principium* if it is to get involved with the alien.

The present study does not seek to cover the alien problematics in all of its daunting entirety. It only identifies some basic motifs that inspired the author to develop a phenomenology of the alien with a special series of books on the alien. The first volume of the series came out in 1990 under the title *The Sting of the Alien* (*Der Stachel des Fremden*).[1] Motifs are the moving powers which push matters forward, instead of merely providing retroactive justification for having addressed them. There is no sufficient justification or explanation for the experience of the alien, just as there is none for wonder, terror, love, hate, or those miniature disruptions which announce the arrival of something new. The individual chapters of this book are designed in such a way as to address a particular programmatic component of alien problematics. Their order corresponds to the individual phases in which the phenomenology of the alien has taken shape; they can thus be read as introductory or explanatory supplementary texts for the more extensive studies that have already seen light. The following section connects this work with the earlier ones, thus sparing me the need to engage in detailed individual referencing and allowing me to focus on the core questions. The key themes here are as follows: order – pathos – response – body – attention – interculturality.

Chapter 1 is closely related to the preliminary examination of *Order in the Twilight* (*Ordnung im Zwielicht*, 1987). At the limits of every order, the alien emerges in the shape of something extraordinary that cannot find its place in the respective order, and, at the same time, as what is being excluded, it is not nothing. Since it is not excluded as such, but is rather excluded from a specific order, the alien signifies more than the gray-on-gray of mere indeterminacy. Since it appeals to our senses, it expresses more than just the noise from which we shield ourselves as much as we can. This initial position which confronts us when we encounter the ungraspable in the graspable, the unordered in the ordered, the invisible in the visible, the silent in the audible, transforms into a chain of investigations, all of which gather around the question: how can we engage the alien without already neutralizing or denying its effects, its challenges and demands in and through the way of dealing with the alien? As a phenomenologist, I have always been careful to avoid doing that regarding which an impatient audience likes to accuse phenomenologists of the alien, namely, elevating the alien to the status of some moral or religious authority or putting it on the pedestal of an "entirely other." Giving in to this temptation would mean that a divinization of the Other—an accusation often raised against Levinas—finds its counterpart in the moralization of the alien. However, an experience can be coerced just as little as, according to Kant, a feeling can be. Not that the experience of the alien would be a merely subjective feeling, as modernity would prescribe; it is just that there are many more things in this world than a school doctrine with its norms, values, and interests can possibly imagine.

Experiences can be treated with a different degree of care; one can let them speak for themselves, use them as an information resource, or make an attempt at silencing them, be it out of negligence, power play, or mere indifference. Chapters 2 and 3 treat these possibilities from the perspective of a responsive ethics, i.e., an ethics which emerges from responding, thus staying behind the level of commandments and prohibitions. Here, the pre-predicative experience in the Husserlian sense is transformed into a pre-normative experience which is always already left behind when one sketches out future actions or makes life plans that require some moral or legal assessment. In chapter 2, I mainly refer to *The Jagged Lines of Experience* (*Bruchlinien der Erfahrung*, 2002). The examinations undertaken in that text revolve around a double event, which consists of a preceding pathos and a subsequent response. Therefore, in the beginning there is what happens to us and confronts us as the events in which myself or the Other may participate, and not as a willful subject who performs acts or commits deeds. Decisive here is the temporal shift, the *diastase*. The bottom line is not that *something* precedes the initiative of the self, but that this initiative precedes *itself* and does not simply start in itself. These connections appear in a new light when, in chapter 3, closely following the *Response Register* (*Antwortregister*, 1994),[2] I develop the basic features of responsive behavior and a correlative responsive logic as it emerges from the call of the alien. The paradox of creative responding makes for a special case. It turns out that we indeed can take the "what" of the response as something invented, but we cannot do the same with the "to what" of responding. The call of the alien can be just as little associated with ethical fundamentalism as it can be with technological constructivism.

Chapter 4, which is concerned with corporeal experience, is by no means a mere extension of the alien sphere. In the nexus of self-reference and self-withdrawal that designates its mode of being, the body proves to be an emblem of the alien, as it were. Alienness does not start with myself; otherwise, it would not mean much. The so-called subject loses its central position when it presents itself as *Embodied Self* (*Leibliches Selbst*)— the title of the lectures on the body which were published in 2000 and which treat this thematic in all its depth. In a refined form, chapter 5 presents the basic ideas, supported by literary works, of *The Phenomenology of Attention* (*Phänomenologie der Aufmerksamkeit,* 2004). The latter is entirely attuned to the double rhythm of becoming apparent and becoming attentive; the double movement of pathos and response thereby acquires a specific shape that penetrates all our experience and behavior. What becomes apparent or comes to our mind, what comes to our eyes, or our ears, i.e., our senses, comes toward us; it is not our own. This allusion to the title *Thresholds of Sense* (*Sinnesschwellen,* 1999) points to the fact that the omnipresent phenomenon of attention leads us into the region of *aesthesis,* i.e., of modern aesthetics, but also the area of a peculiar ethos of the senses. Intimated in the latter two chapters are also the alien aspects of both psychoanalysis and technology, which take up significant space in *The Jagged Lines of Experience* and *The Phenomenology of Attention.* Just as the most primordial experience is permeated by moments of the unknown and unmotivated, so too the phenomena of experience are from the start marked by a genuine phenomenotechnology and somato-technology. Technology, which has for a very long time—despite all the contemporary lamentations about alienation through technology—been regarded as an extension of the sphere of ownness, now proves more and more to be a source of alienation of its own kind.

Chapter 6 can be read as a recapitulation, which gathers different aspects of the alien in a summary oriented toward a relationship between cultures. Interculturality does not stop short at the borders of philosophy.[3] A global thinking is neither to be expected nor to be desired since it would inevitably form another hegemonic relationship, only by different means. However, it might be a relief to have philosophy stop revolving around itself and take root in the all too familiar culture. The effort of crossing borders without eliminating them is one of the future adventures of interculturality that means more than a multicultural juxtaposition or intermingling. Mere multiplicity too easily turns into an accumulation that might provide entertaining and promising variation, but fails to disrupt our slumber. The danger for the cultures that have come of age is the recourse to the hunter-gatherer society.

The current book is based on a series of individual studies which owe their emergence to diverse occasions. All these studies were revised and oriented toward the common theme of this book.[4] A retroactive systematization has been avoided in order to preserve the heuristic plurality of approaches. At the same time, what I have aimed at is the formation of reliefs, which would allow for essential aspects to come into view like mountain chains in a pop-up card. As writers, we sometimes regret that writing happens merely on a two-dimensional plane; fortunately, writing has its own modes of emphasis, and so does reading. These ups and downs prevent the *ductus* of writing, which supplies writing with a peculiar shape of alienness, from flattening out into something that is merely written.

1

The Human as a Liminal Being

The alien is a limit phenomenon par excellence. It arrives from else-where, even when it appears in our own house and own world. There can be no alien without an alien place. How much weight is given to the alien will thus depend on the kind of order in which our life, our experience, our language, our acts and deeds take shape. When the order becomes transformed, there is also a transformation of the alien which is as multi-faceted as the orders which it transcends. The expression "the alien" is no less occasional than the expression "the ego." The limit zones which expand between and beyond the orders are the breeding grounds for the alien.

1. Orders and Their Limits

We are usually right to assume that orders do not merely have boundaries, but that boundaries emerge from ordering processes. Something is what it is by virtue of its separation from other things: stones, plants, animals, or human beings, natural or artificial things. However, when it comes to the human realm, the concept of boundary is a particularly restless one, because boundaries are constantly in question. The human being is characterized by the fact that its behavior is brought to certainty neither by instinctive regulations nor by some artificial programs; it is a creature that is not locked in by fixed boundaries, but rather relates to these boundaries in a certain manner. That goes for the limits of place and time, which define our concept of here and now, for the limits imposed by various prohibitions, which restrain our desires and deeds, and for the limits of understanding, which curb our thoughts. Therefore it is no wonder that the question of the limits of existence and those of the world should be found among the major themes in human history, be it Jehovah, who separates light from darkness, be it the immeasurable boundaries of the soul, be it the modern philosopher, who maps out the boundaries of pure reason, or be it the systems theorist, who presents the sublime gesture of creation in a minimalist formula: "Draw a distinction!"

This already indicates that drawing boundaries, which leads to different sorts of orders and structures, does not merely have a pragmatic and regional, but also an epochal character. It may be assumed that every epoch (more specifically: every culture, society, environment, or form of life) behaves within certain boundaries, but that the relation to the boundaries, which is always accompanied by a certain politics, is subject to significant variations. The ways one handles boundaries serve as a clear indication of the underlying spirit of an epoch; it may also provide a commentary on that which has advanced modernity for such a long time, including what had preceded it or undermined and transgressed it. That the recently crossed threshold which leads us into the new century is definitely a very particular boundary is as true as the fact that we do not have a suitable language for that which lies ahead of us.

2. Boundless Universe

For the sake of contrast, let us begin with the boundless universe, represented in our cultural tradition most succinctly by the Greek cosmos. The cosmos depicts a classical form of order, because it had played a paradigmatic role for a long period of time. The cosmos does not embody one order among a range of other possible orders; it embodies order as such. The only alternative to it is the unordered manifold of chaos. In this cosmos each being is given its own limited shape (πέρας), the boundaries of which *delimit* this being for itself and from its surroundings. The clear-cut shape is expressed in the conceptual definition (ὁρισμός); since the times of Plato, it has been dialectics that related each being as the same to its other in a nexus of relations. This horizontal nexus is complemented by a vertical hierarchy, the proportions of which correspond to the degree to which the rational whole is reflected in the individual being. In that sense, the humans would stand above the animals, the Greeks above the barbarians, the man above the woman, the contemplation above the action. The participation in rationality, which discloses the law of the whole, is decisive for where one stands in the hierarchy of individual beings.

This relational structure, which has all difference as relative, features a lower and an upper boundary. The lower boundary is formed by the *in-dividual,* an ἄτομον εἶδος, which cannot be divided into further entities without destroying its identity. The upper boundary is formed by the universe, a ἓν καὶ πᾶν, which itself cannot be ordered into or under anything else; the world is an entity "from which nothing is excluded," as is stated in Aristotle's *Physics* (3.6.207a8). To put it simply: the cosmos is an *order without an outside;* all it has are internal boundaries. The one who crosses these boundaries either enters the bad infinity of the end-less, bottomless, and pointless *apeiron* or raises himself to the extreme heights like Icarus, whose attempt to conquer the heavens ended in a fatal crash.

However, the idea of a closed and all-embracing cosmos that pro-vides a suitable place for each being and prefigures its paths is based on the implicit assumption that the place where the whole shows and ex-presses itself *as a whole* is still thought of as a place *within that whole* itself. The psyche, which is, according to Aristotle, "in some sense everything," becomes the stage of the very order to which it mimetically adjusts itself. The cosmos thus appears as an order which unveils and expresses *itself as itself* by changing all conditions into moments of itself. This order with-out an outside corresponds to a *thought of the inside,* a *penser du dedans,* to modify Foucault's famous title, and on the whole this thought would be by itself. Yet even the ancient Greeks knew of the figures who did not fit this scheme, for example, Socrates, this ἄτοπος, who lives in the city with other fellow citizens but acts as a living question mark, or the Platonic *ma-nia* of poetry and eros, or the Sophists, who counter the true logos with the artificial trick and techniques of *lexis,* or a tragic figure like Oedipus, who sees only when he becomes blind, chained to his ominous fate, which isolates him and labels him as a homeless person (ἄπολις).[1] Such marginal figures, whose anomaly makes normality less secure, are also found in other places. For example, mystical sidestreams tend to accom-pany the main stream of unquestionable devotion to law and text, casting a shadow of heterodoxy and anarchy. This holds for both the Jewish or Islamic traditions, but also for the Christian tradition. Even Saint Paul dissociates himself from the kind of rhetoric in which the γλῶσσα or the *lingua* loosen the tongue to the extent that allows it to escape either the individual or public control. The saying, which evaporates in the cosmos of the said, is replaced with the saying, which says *no thing* and which is in that sense meaningless. The charismatic, which Max Weber opposes to the everyday life of institutions, pervades everything; it also serves as an indication that any normality, even the cosmologically, theologically, or cosmopolitically simulated normality, omits something which then finds an expression in anomalies and frays into some *lunatic fringe.*

3. Ownness, Alienness, Contingency

A global order is not conceivable without a rupture, unless the place from which the whole unfolds, evaporates in a specific whole. What we call modernity can be described as the movement to question the vision of the whole. The self-deception of a *kosmotheoros,* who reckons himself as a part of the scene he beholds, is breached, and the pretended order turns out to result from an establishment of order [*Ordnungsstiftung*]. The two key discoveries here are (1) the discovery of a *self* that says "I" before it is named "subject," and, as a result of its self-referentiality, the relational structure of the whole explodes, and (2) the discovery of a radical *contingency* that does not only utilize the open places of an order, but affects the order itself. Such an order can not only degenerate into disorder but can also become a different order; it can be different from itself. For example, in Descartes' cogito one not only finds the pinnacle of thought but also the idea that God could have created a different mathematics. The orders in which we move turn out to be merely potential orders. As the strange protagonist in Musil's *Man Without Qualities* suspects, even God prefers to speak of the world in the weaker form of a *conjunctivus potentialis:* "for God makes the world and while doing so thinks that it could just as easily be some other way" (Musil 1961, 15). The fact that for the young Ulrich this suspicion is linked to the thesis that "anyone who really loved his country should never think his own country the best" (ibid.) gives the matter a political flavor. The decisive factor here is that the motifs of subjectivity and rationality, which cause us trouble even in the present, act as a double motif. The modern subject appears as a being that is looking for its place but does not have it, and that can no longer act as a substitute for a single rationality.

If this double motif is to be considered seriously, in all its radicality, the problem of drawing boundaries should also change. Then the self, which lives in its own sphere and conforms to its own cultural order, even for language and the senses, will no longer be reducible to something same that is separate from the other in the context of universality. Selfness and ownness are the results of drawing boundaries that distinguish an inside from an outside and thus adopt the shapes of *inclusion* and *exclusion.* Ownness arises when something withdraws from it, and exactly that which withdraws is what we experience as alien or heterogeneous. This separation of the *own* and the *alien,* effected by no third party, belongs to a different dimension than the distinction between *same* and *other,* which is backed by a dialectically created whole. Or to put it in the mother tongue of Western philosophy: the other (ἕτερον) and the alien (ξένον) are two different things. The alienness of a guest, and this includes the Stranger from Elea who makes an appearance in Plato's *Sophist,* of another language and of another culture, the strangeness of the other sex or that of "another state" can by no means be reduced to the fact that something or someone appears to be different. Building materials such as wood and concrete, or types of wine such as Beaujolais and Rioja, are indeed different from one another, but no one would claim that they are alien to one another. Alienness presupposes that a self (*ipse*) should have a sphere of ownness and its own being, and that this self should not be confused with the same (*idem*), which is discernable by a third party.

4. Modern Compromises

Nietzsche writes: "I think it is important to get rid of *the* universe, the unity. . . . We should smash the universe; unlearn our respect for it" (*KSA* 12: 317). No one could say that modernity ever got serious about the consequences of delimiting orders. Up until today we have tended toward compromises, in which the mutual contamination of self and same and of other and alien has played a significant role. The ambivalences of assessing a new ordering potential affect also the most recent conflict between the representatives of modernity and postmodernity. Consider the motif of a self that says "I" and thus dissociates itself from the whole. The "I" literally means an exception. Connecting the Cartesian ego directly to egocentricity would make things too easy. It would also neglect the restlessness that speaks from this radical self-reflection, the very restlessness that pushes the philosopher to search for an unshakable foundation. Though this search is bound to failure, the question remains "What motivates it, this search?" Even if the question "*Who* am I?" happens to revert all too quickly to "*What* am I?," this strange question, which short-circuits the questioner and the questioned, already contains a trace of Rimbaud's "JE est un autre."

However, be that as it may, the discovery of a self, whose selfness separates it from the relational structure of a natural and social universe, is diluted if it is turned into a mere *particularity*. At the end, we would be confronted only with the conflict between *individualism* and *holism*, between *particularism* and *universalism*, a conflict that still lingers but has never accomplished much. Since a whole cannot be conceived without having any parts in which it articulates itself, and since general regulations are of little use without the particular circumstances to which they apply, the conflict leads to a great coalition where the Aristotelians are seated next to the Kantians, the hermeneuts next to the universal pragmatists. However, this harmony is easily unsettled: one would only have to remind oneself of the fact that the origin of "I-You-Here-Now" does not at all designate the elements that belong to general conceptual categories. Rather, these indexical or occasional expressions are demonstrative words that refer to the place of speaking, a place that opens up fields of experience, language, and action before it itself can be subjected to a determination of place. The place that is spoken about does not coincide with the place of speaking, and the same goes for the moment in time. Even as someone who says "I," I am not a countable element of a class or a member of a whole. The "I" of speaking, which is clearly distinguishable from the "I" of the content of what is said, is not a countable thing that could just be put in the plural, and the same goes for the "you." It should thus be understood that within ancient Greek thought, "I" and "we" do not play a thematic role, except in the initial concept of "for us" (πρὸς ἡμᾶς), which tends to be elevated into an existence "on one's own" (καθ᾽αὑτό). The explosive power of the I-speech is equally lost, if the "I" is reduced to a general I-function. Here we need to protect Descartes against his transcendental-philosophical heirs.

The same plight besieges the second discovery, which ascribes an irremovable contingency to all orders. If the *ability to be different* or the *ability to act differently* is seen as a larger or smaller kind of *arbitrariness,* then this interpretation calls for *necessity* as an antipode. With respect to legitimacy claims, this leads us to the conflict between *relativism* and *universalism,* whose weapons have now become as worn out as those that are used in the conflict that we have mentioned above. Once again a simple fact should be remembered. The establishment of orders with their legitimacy, including the genealogy of true and false, of good and evil, is neither relatively nor absolutely valid. It is not at all valid, since the fact that there are binary standards is not itself subject to these standards, unless their genesis is once again concealed and the respective opposition is hypostatized. Each order has its blind spot in the form of something unordered that does not merely constitute a deficit. That goes for moral orders as well as for cognitive and aesthetic orders. This explains why modern authors struggle so hard with the *incipit* of their novels; from the very first step both the writer and the reader walk into the trap of a ready-to-use order.[2] This order testifies that "there are orders"; this term "there are" outruns all attempts of justification, as it is a basic assumption of any such attempt, the zero ground. In other words: the fact of reason is not in itself reasonable. What is currently called postmodernity could mean, among other things, that some battlegrounds have lost their significance—which does not guarantee that the problems which originate from modern subjectivity and rationality would not reoccur at another place.

5. Paradoxes of Self-Bounding

It is no secret that nowadays paradoxes are *en vogue*. Paradoxes are, lit-erally, opinions that conflict with the prevailing opinion (παρὰ δόξαν). Like all "para"- cases (compare parasite, paraphysics, paralogism, para-psychology), paradoxes presume a normal state of things. But as long as paradoxes only deviate from the prevailing opinions, they can be de-fended against any kind of opposition. Things are different when an as-sumption conflicts with its *own* preconditions, making one assumption stronger at the expense of the other and vice versa. In order to prevent assumptions from failing, it is often attempted to downplay paradoxes, as is the case with the famous paradox of the lying Cretan. The distinction between object- and meta-language makes it impossible for a statement to fail because the event of saying, *énonciation,* can no longer be a part of the content of what is being said, *énoncé.* However, this methodological solution is based on the aforementioned bounding, which comes from the outside; it requires a distinction between two levels of speech. The analysis and its solution are situated at the level of what is being said. This means to neglect the possibility of saying and self-saying, which presents itself in what is being said, but without being announced. We encounter self-referentiality in speech acts such as "I promise you that . . . ," lead-ing, for example, to the fact that the Cretan always involves himself in whatever he is talking about. Also, the well-known distinction between the content plane and the relation plane as we know it from the theory of communication by Paul Watzlawick cannot be simply applied *to* speech, since this very distinction is always found *in* speech.

Something similar occurs in the case of self-bounding, where that which bounds itself is a result of the act of bounding—not as in the event of a third party that separates one thing from another without getting in-volved in this separation itself (see page 81). The fungi expert is neither poisonous nor edible, just like the judge qua judge has no part in the deeds of the accused or the damages incurred by the plaintiff. However, what happens when someone apologizes, or "is devoured by regret"? It is easy to think of those examples where we encounter something strange, from which someone bounds *himself* and his own, without there being any *third party.* Think of the difference between nearness and remote-ness in time and space, as in the distinctions between here and there, now and then, or once upon a time; think of the alternating worlds of waking and sleeping; think of contacts with the dead as in the uncanny "conversations with the dead" that leap over the gap of memory in Juan Rulfo's novel *Pedro Páramo;*[3] think of interpersonal relations like those between man and woman, between child and adult; think of social exclusions on account of class, profession, and culture; or, finally, think of the boundaries of normality that separate the healthy from the ill, the innocent from the criminal, the orthodox from the heretics, the insiders from the outsiders. In all these cases, the one who ascribes to himself either of both states, or feels himself belonging to either of both domains, will find himself on one side of the threshold. And the transitions like falling asleep or waking up, becoming ill or getting well, getting old, being retrained or being converted, do not mean that one adopts a different or neutral position, but rather that one becomes someone other. To what an extent awakening relies on merely corporeal self-orientation is shown by Proust, whose *Recherche* starts at the threshold of waking and sleeping. This and similar experiences, where the own is confronted with the alien, are border-crossing experiences par excellence and, as we will see, also involve a doubling movement. The double nature of bounding, in which, on the one hand, one is separated from the other, and, on the other hand, certain regions are delimited, allows for further differentiation.

The first aspect concerns the self-referentiality of the activity of bounding off. The operative boundary is not anything simply found or drawn by someone. In this respect, the line drawn on the blackboard is misleading. The act of drawing a boundary, which takes place when something separates itself from another, can be neither seen nor touched; it can only be grasped as a trace of drawing a boundary. The act of drawing a boundary can thus be compared to the act of making a contract, an act which does not become a part of the contract itself, yet which becomes tangible indirectly through a change in one's responsibilities. The act of drawing a boundary takes place at a zero point which lies neither at the hither side nor beyond the boundary. The operative boundary is thus neither a definable thing, nor nothing, since without this boundary there would be neither this nor that; likewise, there would be neither I nor others. *The self-referentiality of drawing boundaries consists in its self-withdrawal.*

The second aspect concerns the self-referentiality which appears in the *self* of self-bounding and which leads to inbounding and outbounding. This self is neither the veiled subject of one's own act of bounding, nor the objective result of an alien act of bounding, but within the act of bounding it springs out, as it were; it appears as a cavity, as an *inside which separates itself from an outside* and thus produces a *preference in the difference*. Formally speaking, this means that that *which* separates itself is being marked, while that *from which* it separates itself remains unmarked. In this lies an irreducible asymmetry, without which there would be no self that could adopt the viewpoint of another or a third party. This one-sidedness, which is inherent in the contrast between the own and the alien, can be illustrated by the aforementioned examples. The "here" and "now" that separates itself from the distance, the past, and the future, belongs to the distinction; at the same time, the "here" and "now" presents itself as the very place where this distinction occurs. The same goes for any other distinction. We are not dealing with a neutral, disembodied, gender-free, or ageless third party that could differentiate between man and woman, between adult and child; nor is there a trans-national or transcultural third party that could set the Germans against the French, or the Europeans against the Asians. The Germans much rather distinguish *themelves* from the French, like female beings distinguish *themselves* from male beings, and he or she who distinguishes him- or herself in this way can only become who he or she really is through this distinction. Whoever distinguishes (or separates) himself or herself is on one side; the alien or strange, in the sense of that from which he or she separates himself or herself, is on the other side. *The reference to the alien lies in the withdrawal of the alien.* The fact that this asymmetry doubles and multiplies certainly does not lead to a symmetry. The *syn-* of symmetry depends on the fact that the own and the alien are subject to a common point of view or a common rule. The "equalization of the non-equal" mentioned in Nietzsche's *On Truth and Lie in a Nonmoral Sense* posits as equal what *is* not equal. Normalization as a selective form of ordering, which begins already in the orthoaesthesia of the senses, cannot be conceived of without the shadow of the heteroaesthesia, and the same goes for orthodoxy, orthology, and orthopraxis.[4]

The paradox of self-referentiality is further strengthened by the fact that the first aspect of self-referential bounding off and the second aspect of bounding oneself in and bounding the alien out dovetail into each other in the form of a *reference to the alien within the self-reference.* As a result of the inevitable self-thematizing, the self enters the ordering net that it designs. The "here" of the body can be located, for example, by the red arrow on the street map which shows the position of its user. Likewise, the "now" can have a date and be marked in the calendar. The body, which will be addressed in detail in a subsequent chapter, reveals itself as a lived body, which continuously evades the reflections of consciousness and resists our initiatives. A similar thing takes place on the social level that comes in the form of intercorporeality. The "I" without which there would be no other is described by Husserl in the *Crisis* as a "privileged member" (*Hua* VI:188; *Crisis,* 185); yet, at the same time, the "I" discovers itself as an ordinary member of a group that it helps to constitute. The "I" is an Other because alienness begins in one's own house. The alien reference within the self-reference explains why no one is merely who they are, and causes the chain of self-doubling that occurs under different circumstances in the works of Husserl and Merleau-Ponty, as well as Foucault and Luhmann. These doublings should not be confused with reflections of a reflexive self-consciousness, which is simultaneously a subject and an object; neither are they related to the intersubjective dialectics of recognition, wherein one subject finds itself in another subject. The corporeal self-withdrawal, which becomes clear in the difference between functioning and thematizing, much rather corresponds to the difference between expressing and expression, between saying and what is said, when we consider the fact that the event of saying something can never be exhausted by what is said. From a more general point of view we can say that this kind of restlessness, which leads to continuous self-doublings, springs from the fact that the place where boundaries are drawn is situated neither inside nor outside the orders, but both inside and outside at the same time. Self-withdrawal means that certain moments of the alien in the self, those moments of the alienness in the given order, are virulent. The double play, as Foucault shows, turns into a trompe l'oeil if one continues to try catching up with the seeing in the seen, with the saying in the said, with the thinking in the thought, instead of thinking of these doublings as a part of the game itself.

6. Possibilities and Impossibilities

The kind of thinking which surrenders to the paradoxes of a self-bounding and thus self-exceeding order produces a number of thinking patterns that do not fit into the framework of traditional thinking. *Deviations* from an order, which play an important role not only in modern poetics but also in the self-organization of nature, do not show that there is something that deviates because deviance springs rather from the self-deviation of vision or speech, which escape from themselves. Another thinking pattern is that of the *surplus*. The kind of speaking and acting that moves along the boundaries of their respective orders lags behind itself as it brings more possibilities into the game than it can employ, on the one hand, and on the other hand, it goes beyond itself as it touches upon the impossibilities of the invisible, the unheard, and the unthought. The more and the less of meaning belong to the forms of a nonclassical art and are indicative of a surplus or lack of sense, which finds no place in the classical patterns of the fulfillment of desires and commands. As the "non-fixated animal" which finds itself forced to invent and create orders, man reveals himself as a lack-being and, at the same time, a surplus-being. He cannot rely on anything, not even on natural or essential needs, and he cannot concentrate on any fixed goals, not even on regulative ideas, which require a unified standard. "There are orders," and this flexible basic fact refers to those orders that are indeed subject to necessary and restrictive conditions, for which, however, no sufficient reasons can be found. Orders create possibilities and impossibilities, but something that is not made possible is the institution [*Stiftung*] of new orders. Here we find a moment of factual unconditionality amidst experience. Radically alien is exactly that which cannot be anticipated by any subjective expectations or by any trans-subjective conditions for possibilities. The surplus of experience, which leads us beyond the existing orders, finally joins a spatiotemporal *shift*, based on the fact that the self-reference never returns to itself, that—as we have seen—the place or time of speech never coincides with the place or time which is being spoken about. Self-withdrawal means that something is there by being absent, that something is near by moving far away. This shift starts with one's own birth, which is never fully one's own, as it is never actively experienced and is never a subject of free choice. My involvement with my own past is expressed playfully by Laurence Sterne, who delays the birth of his hero Tristram Shandy again and again, yet, at the same time, anticipates it in such impossible phrases as "I am not yet born" (1950, 33). Carlo Levi wrote about this: "Tristram Shandy non vuol nascere, perché non vuol morire" (quoted from Italo Calvino, *Lezioni Americane,* 1988, 46). The birth concerns me, and yet I cannot attribute it to myself like an act that I myself have completed. Each birth is a premature one, and each infant is a latecomer, and this delay repeats itself wherever anything new that breaks through the existing measures comes into being. Each new forming thus reveals itself as a *reforming* of existing formations. A first speech and a first act are therefore as impossible as a last word and a last deed. An "absolute present," which would gather in it all sense, belongs to the phantasms of traditional orders that deny their origin.

The alien that exceeds the playing field of possibilities as something extra-ordinary can therefore be regarded as something im-possible, and not in the sense of an ontological, epistemical, practical, or logical impossibility, but in the sense of a lived impossibility.[5] In the above two instances the hyphen indicates that that which exceeds the orders does not lead into a yonder world, but a beyond of this world. However, the question of the possibilities and impossibilities of experience, speech, and deeds shows an ambiguity with which our considerations reach their extreme point. The question that emerges at this point concerns the aforementioned relation between self-reference and reference to the alien.

The reference to the alien can be interpreted in two ways, as a *boundary* of one's own capacities or as a *questioning of the own.*

Hermeneuts like Gadamer or pragmatists like Rorty who rely on belonging to a tradition hold a vague intermediary position. The alien is included in the conversation, but only to the extent that it also belongs to it, such that any questioning of the own turns into a questioning of the own by the own. One keeps to oneself. It does not make a big difference whether a strong faculty of reason is attributed to the tradition, or a weaker one is at play, as in Gianni Vattimo's sense. With other theoreticians, the matter is more unequivocal. We find the first interpretation of the alien reference in the system theory of Niklas Luhmann, who is persistent yet flexible in reflecting upon how to deal with boundaries, but who always halts at a specific boundary. For him, the reference to the alien means a self-reference that underwent a temporal shift. Each observation that means something, thereby distinguishing it from other things, can itself become the subject of an observation by oneself or another. The only thing that remains strange is the *operatio pura* of the observer, which vaguely reminds us of the *actus purus* of Aristotelian theology. The blind spot of observation is not erased but wanders from one systemic position to another. In contrast to communicative reason, which always involves the strange into something common, systemic reason leaves room for alienness. However, this alienness means nothing more than *excluded, yet, under certain conditions, (re)includable possibilities.* Such *alienness* merely marks boundaries of ability, which can be one's own, a common, or an operative ability. In this way, the self-reference holds primacy even when accessing the self meets clear boundaries. This primacy turns into its pure opposite when the self submits to an alien power and therefore recognizes the alien as its unconditional master. It seems as if both extremes of a *functionalist misjudgment* of the alien and a *fundamentalist idealization* of the alien strove to strengthen each other. The fleeting game with possibilities would then be opposed to a new compact reality, as is already indicated in Musil's Kakania. Moral observers and moralists give each other a lot to do, since both are after stabbing each other in the back. The moral observer is reminded of his observational morality, the moralist is reminded of his hidden amorality. This, too, predicts a long-term struggle which is practiced all too explicitly on objects like the holocaust memorial.

Is that all? Do the boundaries of orders admit of nothing but an antithesis, nothing but a polemic complementarity of self-reference and alien reference? An alternative, which corresponds to the second form of alien reference, would be the return to a *self-reference within the reference to the alien,* with a new form of responsivity that allows for the inevitability of demands to be combined with the creation of our own answers. As we are going to see next, this very im-possibility can also go back to the demands of the alien, which thwart our own ideas and desires, and break through common rules. The resistance of the alien results from the absence of any equivalent, including a moral equivalent, which escapes from the order. For every order, the alien remains an alien intruder.

2

Between Pathos and Response

If we presume that the alien transgresses the boundaries of every order, the question arises as to what an experience in which such a transgression takes place would be like. It is not to be expected that a combination of sense and rule, of the intentional and rule-guided acts of a subject, along with the consensual agreement between different subjects, can stand up to the challenges of the alien. The alternative envisioned here appears in a form of phenomenology which is grounded in pathos and directed toward responsivity; yet this alternative takes us to the margins of a particular kind of phenomenology and hermeneutics, aiming merely at the interpretation of sense.

1. In the Realm of Sense

Similarly to Freud, who introduces the unconscious as the shibboleth of psychoanalysis, one could say that intentionality is the shibboleth of phenomenology. In its precise definition, intentionality means that *something* shows itself *as something*,[1] that something is meant, given, understood, or treated in a certain way, namely, the green of new grass, a bloodstain, the taste of strawberries, a table, a Pegasus, an Arabic number, a love letter, a computer text program, a feverish infection, an attack, a terrorist act, and so on. The formula *something as something* means that something (actual, possible, or impossible) is linked to something else (a sense, a meaning) and is at the same time separated from it. Reality and sense cannot be set against each other like characteristics or values. Like a fugue which connects the unconnected, the miniature "as" marks a broken connection. Merleau-Ponty speaks of a zero point, joint, or fold that characterizes the emergence of sense and Gestalt. The "as" does not form a third entity which pushes between two initial realities of which one is real and the other ideal, or of which one is physical and the other psychic. Rather, it marks a dynamic structure without which there would literally be nothing which shows itself, and thus nobody to whom something appears. Nothing is given without being given *as such,* and nobody responds to it without acting *as somebody.* Leaning in on that aspect of this differentiating process, which generates meaning, I have often spoken of *significative difference*. In comparison with the basic character of this differentiating process, the recourse to acts of endowment with meaning appears as a specific interpretation. The fact that I notice a slip of the tongue, a note on the door, or a strange sound from an engine does not yet have the character of an act which I attribute to myself.

If we hold on to the genuine differentiating character of the doctrine of meaning, there are not only connections across the different versions of phenomenology, but also links to a hermeneutics of *Dasein*, to the interpretation of traditions and texts, to semiotic approaches, and, last but not least, to analytic philosophy, following Frege and Wittgenstein. This makes the idea of a paradigm shift in phenomenology from the philosophy of consciousness to semantics, as proposed by Ernst Tugendhat, much less plausible. Despite all the differences and discrepancies between the alternatives mentioned here, something common comes to the fore, leading to a philosophy of sense. In turn, the latter brings the usual epistemological fights, like the one between realism and idealism, to a dead end, simultaneously ending the tug of war between subject and object. The division into outer and inner worlds, which was introduced by John Locke and reintroduced repeatedly after him, calls for a complementary third world of ideas, as it has proved to be a construction which leaves the ground of experience before it has even found it. An experience imbued with intentionality takes place neither inside nor outside. Similarly, the separation of empirical data and general ideas comes to be undermined. As with the formation of sense and Gestalt, from the beginning, experience tends toward generalization, without relying on data for its basis. The "as" and "how" inherent in intentionality imply the possibility of repetition and thus an ideality in a genetic and operative sense, prior to all eidetic or categorial intuition. In other words, an intentional and differential experience brings about a multiplicity of horizontal and vertical mediations, without relying on a ready-made reason or a directing subject. Rather, reason and subject themselves undergo a genesis. Phenomenology with the concept of a sense- and experience-horizon institutes a liminal concept par excellence and deals in its own way with the question of how limits can be described and transgressed without being eliminated.

Thinking within and at the limits of experience, which was discussed in the first chapter, also stems from the basic position which we have designated as the shibboleth of phenomenology, for it only takes a small step to endow the *something as something* with the coefficient of contingency. The fact that something appears as something means *eo ipso* that it appears *only in this and not in a different way*. From the perspective of

Gestalt theory, each sense, which expands as a context of references, is a privileged sense. A plant can be used as a medicine or be left as a weed; a knife can be used for eating or as a weapon; a monetary contribution can be considered as a donation or a bribe; a foreigner can be treated as an asylum seeker or an illegal alien. As was emphasized by Nietzsche, attached to sense is an irrevocable perspectivity but also a potential for conflict. There is sense, but not some single sense; sense develops on the background of non-sense, as Merleau-Ponty shows in his *Phenomenology of Perception* (Merleau-Ponty, 1945, 342; 2002, 345). Therefore phenomenology (as well as hermeneutics) takes on an indexical character throughout. The *origo* of the Here-Now system which Karl Bühler—inspired by Husserl's *Logical Investigations*—chooses as the center point of his *theory of language* does not represent a complex of principles; rather, it forms a field, a field of pointing, which grounds the symbolic field with its expansions of context and decontextualizations. Beyond all everyday constellations of sense, this indexicality harbors certain historical features which reveal epochal changes. Even those events which we usually designate as "establishments" [*Stiftungen*], such as the birth of tragedy, democracy, or geometry, have their *kairos,* their phases of incubation and decision. Their progression cannot be subjected to teleology, even though the proximity of the concept of sense to the traditional concept of goal or purpose makes such attempts tempting.

If we now consider the entire context, I see no reason to give up this fruitful perspective and simply replace it with another. To do so would be rather naive, since it implies a traditional clash of principles or methods. The orientation of sense lies at the basis of different theories of meaning, understanding, and communication; it even plays a role in system-theoretical approaches. It thus cannot be denied without slipping into silence. What cannot be denied, however, is not yet finalized or guaranteed to be impervious to subversions, and what holds for formations of sense holds a fortiori for those validity claims which are grounded in discourse and serve normatively to filter formations of sense. This is never a matter of abrupt oppositions or mere supplementations; rather, we are concerned with the shifts which manifest their sustained effects similarly to the nuances of a color painting.

2. Abysses of the Pathic

The questioning of intentionality must emerge from intentionality itself; as in the case of understanding or communication, one is doomed to fail trying to escape its grasp. A direct confrontation with it would mean to fall back on the givennesses devoid of sense and norms and to pretend there is indeed *something* that could remain unaffected by the prescriptions of sense and norms. The presumption of such a "something" would sooner or later end up in the nets of sense and bound by the chains of argumentation. Following an indication of the basic formula that was chosen for this analysis, there are wrong ways of a special kind, as we must realize as soon as we consider the happening of sense more closely. That something appears *as something* does not mean that it *is something*. It *becomes something* by obtaining a sense and thus becomes sayable, approachable, repeatable. It does not suffice to presume a genesis of sense, as if something merely comes to light from the pits of experience. Rather, it is an accomplishment of sense, a generation of sense, as when one speaks about the generation of energy. In this heterogenesis, which also sheds a new light on heteronomy, something comes into play which does not yet have a sense, and the question is how to grasp this *heteron* as such.

To elucidate this question, let me introduce a scene from Robert Musil, an author who not only was close to Ernst Mach and inspired by Nietzsche but also was familiar with Husserl's early work. Right in the initial passage of *Man Without Qualities,* a Viennese couple is brought to witness an event which we usually describe *as a traffic accident,* just as we designate certain meteorological processes measured by barometric pressure, humidity, and location of the sun *as a gorgeous August day.* Yet this is not true from the beginning. There are some cliffs which can break the flow of events. Everything begins with a "crowd," with a blocked movement. I hear something heavy "spinning sideways, then the sound of abrupt braking, and what appears to be a heavy truck is now sitting with one wheel on the edge of the pavement, stranded." Next to it stands the driver, "grey as the pavement," trying to account for what happened. The gazes of the bystanders sink into the "depth of the enclosed space" where the victim of the accident is lying as if dead. Someone has called the ambulance, the "expert, authorized aid" for which emergency is a normal state of affairs. In the meantime, the "know-it-all" man explains to some woman what it means to have "too long a braking distance." The woman is thankful for these explanations; "it was sufficient for her that in this way the horrible happening could be fitted into some kind of a pattern, becoming a technical problem that would no longer concern her directly." It becomes a case for the "social institutions" which are so admirably accurate in their services. "People walked around with that almost justifiable impression that what had occurred was an event within the proper framework of law and order." The comment of the talkative man and the reaction of the woman, his companion, confirm this impression. " 'According to the American statistics,' the man noted, 'there are over a hundred and ninety thousand people killed on the roads annually over there, and four hundred and fifty thousand injured.' 'Do you think he is dead?' his companion asked, still harboring the unjustified impression that what she had experienced was something exceptional" (Musil 1978, 5–6).

The everyday/non-everyday happening which ends here shows how a tragic event turns into a statistical normality, into an "orderly" event which is endowed with sense and conforms to rules but still leaves behind a subjective feeling as an affect-added value. In the face of an increasing anonymization of that which appears to be most own, this feeling recalls a private relic; eventually we end up with "experiences without the one who has them," as Musil predicts (1978, 150). Of course, this prelude which opens up the journey through Kakania could be pursued further with the help of Foucault or Luhmann, by allowing, for example, the multifunctional system which we call society to show itself with all its agencies of sense. We would find various codes and guiding differences, be they in medical tests, juridical evidence or assessment of action, or insurance agencies; or be they the treatment of incidents in the media, when, depending on the public value of the victim or perpetrator, more attention is given to the fatal accident of the princess than to that of her driver. Finally, there is the literary presentation itself which gains an aesthetics-added value in accordance with the division of labor in this production of sense, and this is without mentioning our own phenomenological gains. The electrical circuit of sense is thus complete.

To be sure, Husserl, in the *Crisis,* makes fun of those who equate the profession of the phenomenologist with that of the proverbial shoemaker who always minds his business (*Hua* VI:140). One could again cite Musil who, through the protagonist's voice, laughs at the situation when "a chicken farm has been created for high-flying thoughts which one refers to as philosophy, theology, or literature" (Musil 1978, 358). The division of professions into specializations, however, should not immediately be sacrificed to some noble humanitarian goal; neither Husserl nor Musil do so, and even less so Max Weber. It might well be that the philosopher and thus also the phenomenologist face certain professional demands as well; yet he should be able and willing to reflect on professionalization in an exemplary fashion. Musil as a literary author owns up to this task; he does not simply relate an accident to arouse the reader's sympathy, but confronts the reader with the transformation of sense which brings about a meaning-ful event. There is something that, when it is well adjusted and otherwise prepared, will in the end fit different "sense provinces." Yet how does this I-don't-know-what emerge which lets itself so easily be presented as this or that? It arises as a surprising event which, like the corpus delicti, "breaks ranks" and "crosses through" an ordinary course of events, arousing attention, attracting the curious like bees, inciting our desire to see, transforming the seeing ones into voyeurs as what has happened to the victim because of his "carelessness."

The accident which the text of this novel reports presents a proto-type for everything which comes to our mind, our attention, which at-tracts, repels, provokes, hurts us, makes us think and, in the worst case, destroys us as a "thinking cane." At this point, we could refer to the phe-nomenology of attention which will be discussed in its own right in a sub-sequent chapter. But what is attention? Does attention have a sense, or is attention just a selective form of intention? This would be the case only if attention is narrowed down in a voluntaristic way or equated with a spotlight which brings to light that which already waits for our gaze in the dark. Yet coming to attention or to mind are no acts which one under-takes or bypasses. Something can come to our attention in the shape of light distractions which appear harmless, but also in the spectacular form of intense disturbances and dangers, as in the case of our traffic victim who—provided he was not suicidal—follows his intentions and is cruelly torn away from them. In order to designate those events which are not at our disposal, as if merely waiting for a prompt or command, but rather happen to us, overcome, stir, surprise, attack us, the old term "pathos" appears appropriate which, through the saying πάθει μάθος, announces a learning through suffering, yet not a learning of suffering.[2] Such a per-spective frees us from the pile-up of subjective, private emotional states which stem from a "complementary abstraction" (*Hua* VI:231; *Crisis*, 226) and serve to compensate, in the shape of psychic data, for what was lost in the reduction of the world to physical data. Two abstractions taken together, however, do not yield a concretion because there is a medium lacking in which they could "grow together." On the other hand, the motif of pathos, which repels such attempts at compensation, is compat-ible with the traditional language of affects and affections, provided we hear in the "at" of af-fects and af-fections a kind of summons, call, ap-peal, as Husserl, Scheler, and Heidegger noted.

Pathos does not mean that there is *something* which affects us, nor does it mean that something is understood and interpreted *as something*. It means both less and more than that; it evades the alternative of cau-sality and intentionality in all its traditional forms.[3] If we count on mere causality, we would have to judge from the perspective of an observer, like the policeman who takes a blood sample, or like the doctor who looks for germs, fights the risk of infection, and determines the cause of death. If we instead rely on pure processes of conceiving, interpreting, and analyzing, it would mean that we have already entered the level of the sense-giving of experience, with the result that the breaking points of experience are concealed by sense-interpreting. Pathos means that we are affected *by something*, in such a way that this "from where" is neither founded on the previous "what," nor can it be sublated into a subsequently accomplished "for what." The different forms of pathos that can be distinguished here are of episodic and chronic kinds, or those which function in a "volcanic" and those which function in a "neptunic" way. In addition, there are different degrees of intensity; as passion, pathos exhibits such strength that it affects everything. The opposite of pathos is not what is counter to sense; nor is it senselessness in the traditional sense which arises from disappointed expectations. Rather, it is apathy or indifference, where it no longer matters whether this or that happens, where everything sinks into the monotony of in-difference, as in the case of Dostoevsky's ridiculous man for whom even reaching for a gun seems to be too much of an effort. Similarly to Leibniz, Husserl uses the metaphor of sleep for such cases; once the "affective relief" (*Hua* XI:168; *ACPAS*, 216) is flattening, an experience goes to sleep. One may wonder whether the metaphor of sleep makes the withdrawal of life appear all too harmless. Even Plato goes a step further when he compares total apathy to the absence of desire in a stone (*Gorgias* 492e).

3. Patient and Respondent

The pathos with which something happens to us disturbs a series of all-too familiar distinctions. This concerns, first, the distinction between subject and object, between objective occurrence and subjective act. Take the classic example of pleasure and pain. These are neither states nor events which could be attributed to the things in the world. Pain without somebody who feels it is only conceivable as a pathological split product, and even that kind of a thing presupposes a minimal connection between the patient and his alienated corporeal state. Pleasure and pain are not subjective acts, however; were they so, the one who suffered from them would have to carry responsibility for them, they could be attributed to him, and they would be embedded in a horizon of understanding. Pathos is an event, but an event of a special kind which happens to *somebody*. The implicated one appears in the dative, in the "address dative," as Bühler (1982, §15) calls this case, and not in the nominative case of the actor; something happens to *me* to which *I* relate in this or that way, and something equivalent happens to *you*. The "from what" of being affected turns into a "to what" of responding as somebody relates to it in a speaking and acting fashion, rejects it, welcomes it, and brings it to expression. The ability "to say what I suffer from," which the poet emphatically declares to be the gift of a god, designates a saying of a special kind in everyday life as well. It is a saying and also a doing which does not begin with itself, but elsewhere, and which therefore always bears traces of some alien influence. The ownness without which nobody would be him- or herself can only come about because of an openness to the alien which nonetheless evades us. It is exactly this which I designate as answering, as response. The entity which bears the title "subject" in the modern era first appears as patient and as respondent, and in such a way that it makes me involved, not as initiator but as somebody who is literally subject to certain experiences, as sub-ject in the unusual sense of the word which both Lacan and Levinas employ. Just as pathos is to be located on the hither side of intentionality, so our response is situated beyond intentionality. Responsivity goes beyond every intentionality because responding to that which happens to us cannot be exhausted in the meaning, understanding, or truth of our response. All this is not restricted to the affective background of our cognitive and practical modes of comportment; it concerns these modes in their essence because whenever something new comes to light in everyday life, or in politics, science, and philosophy, something occurs to us, it comes to our mind, it "dawns" on us. Even history lives because memories are awakened and not just stored and processed like input data. The prestige of computers and robots increases the more cognitions and practices are disaffected, cooled down or frozen, and limited to those achievements which are unaffected by whoever comes to accomplish them. Af-fects, which always harbor some dysfunctional dynamite, turn into a kind of fuel which can be replenished and used up at will. This allows for the construction of feeling machines like Dieter Dörner's EMO machine to which we can attribute emotional movements without emotions, a free adaptation from Musil.[4] Of course, it would be ridiculous to accuse machines of that which essentially belongs to the handling of a machine.

4. On the Hither Side of Good and Evil

A further distinction to be rendered dubious is that between the questions of fact and the questions of right, between "is" and "ought" and also between being and value. What happens to us and unfolds in the varying colors of the horrifying, surprising, attractive, or disturbing neither is a fact which we register nor is it subjected to a norm which we are obliged to follow, nor is it a value or un-value which emerges from our evaluations. Every justification, acceptance, or evaluation is already too late because we are concerned with something which we *nolens volens* presume and have always presumed when we take a position on it in an affirming or denying fashion, highlighting it or crossing it out. In this respect, the described accident proves paradigmatic yet again. It surprises everybody involved even though the usual means of working through and defending get engaged quite soon and so, in the end, only the statistical sand drift remains. Moralizers like to pretend that there could be a complete separation between that which somebody does and that which happens to somebody. Here we observe a tendency to drown suffering in questions of guilt. This began with Job, who had to fend off the accusations of his friends as if they were bothersome flies. The problem here concerns not so much whether the arguers are right; rather, the problem is that even at best they are *merely* right. What happens to us exhibits, on a larger and on a smaller scale, in pleasant as well as in sad and horrible matters, a form of inevitability which the ancient Greeks named *tyche* and which merits in Nietzsche's *amor fati* an antimoralistic outburst.

Husserl has placed special emphasis on the pre-predicative processes that belong to experience because an emerging order of things comes before any explicit "yes" or "no." Similarly, there are pre-normative processes which are certainly not just a part of "word disclosure," that is, a disclosure of sense possibilities. Rather, they speak to us and concern us. These processes provide a hold for normative judgments but not the other way round. Those who overhear and overlook what announces itself here and now will not only fall back behind their own potentialities, but also behind the demands of the alien. The best way to withdraw from moral challenges is to avoid situations in which they can arise. The above-mentioned accident looks comparatively harmless because none of those involved appears particularly challenged in that respect. Yet this is not always the case, and in some senses, it is never the case; even an "uninvolved observer" can be prosecuted for failure to render assistance in the case of an emergency. The way of seeing and thinking which is described here only acquires its appropriate weight when the passivity of that which Husserl calls passive synthesis is not conceived as a mere pre- or lower-level of active sense formations. Rather, it is a radical form of "original passivity" which stems from af-fection and thus continuously imports elements which are "alien to the ego" [*Ichfremdes*]; it is to be attributed to an experience which stems from an occurrence which af-fects me [*Widerfahrnis*]. We thus reach a point where certain events happen for which there are no sufficient conditions for their possibility that can be named. This holds for all establishments [*Stiftungen*] which open up a new realm of sense, be it scientific discoveries, artistic innovations, political or religious reforms, or shifts in philosophical thought. The fact that the emergence of orders manifests itself retroactively in our inventory of orders does not mean that this inventory provides a sufficient hold. After all, dramatic events not only occur in history at large, but also in everyday life where they surprise us as *objets trouvés* and *personnes trouvées* and play their secretive game in the spirit of jocularity, *jeu d'esprit*. Key events of any kind force us to oppose the principle of sufficient reason with a principle of insufficient reason since it can be shown, from case to case, that all attempts at reasoning and justification run up against unsurpassable limits. The question that arises here is how that which evades competent description and explanation can nevertheless be brought into view and expressed. Even the silence in its wake would need to be eloquent if it were to be elucidating.

5. Temporal *Diastasis*

Whenever something happens to us, we exhibit a tendency, which is hard to eliminate, to attribute one part to extraneous causes and the other part to spontaneous acts of freedom, as if we were concerned with the relation between the hammer and the hard place, triumphing or suffering. If there is anything that deters us from this alternative, it would be genuine temporality that determines the double occurrence of pathos and response through and through.

Take once again the above example of a traffic accident. The couple of passersby which comes up in the event making some reassuring comments does not show up until later. "Already a moment earlier, something was out of sync," we hear. Does it mean that the spectators arrived too late? Still, when should they have arrived to catch the event in flagrante? Should they have waited for it like one waits for the sunset? If so, there would have been nothing unusual that had happened; the proverbial *nil novi sub sole* would have to affect the sun itself if habit won out. But how about the perpetrator who struggles for explanations, and how about the victim who causes the incident by his sheer carelessness? The event obviously occurred too early, the response too late—but too early and too late in what respect? Certainly they cannot be measured against the incident itself, for it happens exactly in this temporal lag and nowhere else. The temporality in question does not even come into view if we enter beforehand a dialogical plane where own and alien contributions become synchronized by way of a reciprocity and reversibility of perspectives. In a dialogue, nobody and nothing comes too late because one can always catch up on the basis of joint presuppositions.

I designate the temporal shift which emerges from the antecedence of pathos and the deferment of response, dividing the homogeneous dialogue into a heterogeneous dia-logue, as *diastasis*, that is, as an originary splitting which produces a context, albeit a broken one. The antecedent pathos and the deferred response have to be thought of together, but only across a gap which cannot be closed and thus requires a creative response. Happenings not only lead us to think, they also force us to think. The gap in question is constitutive for the event as much as perspective is constitutive for perception; in this respect, Husserl states that even a perceiving God would be subject to it. Any attempts to resolve the tension in one direction or another by divesting pathos from response or vice versa means taking the pathways of fundamentalism, on the one hand, or those of constructivism, on the other, where one part benefits from minimizing its counterpart. An experience which begins with happenings calls, however, for a different language and also for a different logic. Here, we encounter a curious case where the effect *sub specie patientis* precedes its cause. The linear temporal scheme on which classical physics bases its conception of causality fails if the being-affected retroactively creates a history by reflecting back on the past (see *Hua* X:54). Pathos and response do not follow one after the other like two events; they are not even two distinct events, but one and the same experience, shifted in relation to itself: a genuine time lag. This heterochrony cannot be eliminated by synchronization because the latter already presupposes a temporal *distentio* which dilates every meaningful *intentio*. The spirit of pathos is, in Pascal's words, a "limping spirit" or, more moderately, a delayed spirit. For this reason, we initially do not encounter pathos as *something* which we mean, understand, judge, reject, or affirm; rather, it forms the time-place *from which* we do all this by responding to it. Everything which happens to me and to which I respond does not have a sense as such and does not obey a rule. The insistence on a true surprise, a justified wonder, or a misplaced anxiety imposes criteria on an experience which comes into play only when this experience is being processed. A surprise remains a surprise, wonder remains wonder, anxiety remains anxiety, unless we are confronted merely with ignorance, naiveté, or phantasms, all of which dissolve into nothing as experience is mastered.

Nevertheless, that which disturbs an order is integrated into this order by being named, classified, dated, localized, and subjected to explanations. This reentry, as system theorists call it, which belongs to the effects of happenings and provides them with a certain duration, comes to the fore in Musil's description. But he does more than this: he suspends this normalization by making its effects visible, giving it some ironic shades and thus divesting it of any pretense of prestige. With Musil, we experience how the event disappears behind the "mantle of sense" and slowly acquires a sense, even gains a sense-interest, which allows for speculation and proliferation. The empathetic tone of this irony is less important here than its indirectness, indicating that there is no coincidence between that which is said and understood about the event and that which has happened. The pathos, which is not exhausted in the definition of *pathetique* and which does not even depend on the latter, confronts us with a surplus which can never be entirely consumed. It is something which must be designated as sense- and goal-less because it tears open the nets of sense, interrupts the system of rules, and thus de-contextualizes the event. It is im-mediate only because it breaks through mediations. In order to thematize these irruptions of the pathic, a responsive *epoché* or responsive reduction is required which traces meaning-ful, rule-guided, and value-relevant utterances back to that which calls for their response (see *Antwortregister,* 195). The saying and doing disappear in the meaningfulness and orderliness of what is said and done; this disappearance can only be stopped through a continuous resaying (*redire*) and saying-against (*dédire*), as requested by Levinas (1974, 8–9, 197–98). The coherence of sense and the canon of rules are thus not bypassed but interrupted by the evidence of that which happens to us and forces us to respond. The pathos, which is traditionally associated with the illogical and irrational, is at work in logos itself. A genealogy of logic or morality, which strives to be more than a history of ideas or morals, is only possible if the solid grounds of common sense are left behind, thus returning to reason and freedom its true nature, that of an abyss. For phenomenology, this means the need to turn against itself, to resist the euphoria of sense which would dull it like it dulls other philosophies of sense. Here I see phenomenology's decisive problems; and they do not concern the worn-out heritage of a philosophy of consciousness which can think being-conscious only within the framework of an independent region of consciousness.

6. Testing by Practice

A phenomenology based on pathos and response can be expected to place its own accents in current debates. Below we are going to elaborate on how to envision this with respect to some relevant test cases.

Violence in personal and collective history has been treated by the Judaic-Christian tradition under the heading of evil; in recent times it has been all too readily traced to a general search for meaning or to a moral-juridical assessment. Yet violence comes to light more prominently when it is from the beginning conceived as pathos, injury which happens and is done to somebody. Violence then appears as an alien matter which tears apart the existent structures of meaning.[5] This does not mean that there is nothing here to grasp, to understand, to judge, to repair, and to prevent; but the focal point of all these attempts is not accessible to pseudo-rationalization and one-sided moralization. Even compensation and reparation do not heal the "scars of history." Injuries take on extreme forms in the case of traumatization which blocks or drowns all attempts at a response. Beyond all refusal of discourse there is a silence, a falling into silence, and we make harmless the meaning of this experience by delegating the responsibility for such disturbances to the clinical. In the realm of traumatization, the kind of deferral, the *après coup*, which is characteristic of everything pathic, is encountered in the pathological form of fixating on a happening with the resultant blockage of response. At this point, the phenomenology of time joins the psychoanalytic archeology of pre-time. Finally, not even historiography is exempt from this problem. Past events are forgotten, repressed, and need to be awakened before the archival, monumentalist, or moral work of remembering can be engaged, thus leading to the formation of the so-called culture of remembering. Nietzsche convincingly showed how closely pain and memory, or what has been suffered and what is remembered, are connected. In this respect, Jacob Burckhardt's insistence on embracing the suffering person, in addition to the striving and acting person, in historiology, is almost a public imperative by now, whereas in philosophy, the activism of one-sided theories of action remains prevalent for various reasons.

The bioethical debates can take a different turn if, in the case of birth and death, but also in the case of terminal and life-threatening illness, we begin from an embodied self which has its pre-, post-, and depth-history.[6] This self would, from the beginning, be more than a something to whom certain roles, rights, and capacities are attributed. Monstrous ideas like that of a bunch of cells endowed with dignity would then be revealed as an example of the very same double abstraction discussed above. What happens to the self on the level of the body is multiplied into happenings of happenings when we consider the involvement of the surrounding world, that is, the involvement of all those who, by giving birth, expect the unexpectable, or mourn and say good-bye, in the case of death, to that which evades recollection. Without such pre- and post-histories and without the accompanying interruptions, life would indeed be a product of our doing, even when the *poiema* is potentiated in an *autopoietic* fashion. The old determination of life as self-movement is not entirely false, yet it is insufficient for thinking a self-antecedence, which includes a pathic form of *heterokinesis*.

The debate about the alien will have a chance to liberate itself from the back-and-forth of appropriation and disappropriation, from the attempts to integrate the alien and succumb to the alien, only if the alien is seen from the perspective of pathos as a disruption or disturbance, as in being affected by something which can never be attached to one specific object or meaning. This holds for interpersonal relations just as much as it holds for intra- and intercultural exchanges. The experience of the alien does not begin with either good or bad intentions because it breaks through those expectations of meaning and order on which these intentions are based. Pathos is not merely the unintended, but that which cannot be intended. Philosophically speaking, the alien is something which, in the middle of all potentialities of a personal-dispositional, historical-cultural, or even transcendental kind, proves to be im-possible, a disturbance or challenge to existent possibilities. This points in the direction of that which we find in authors like Bergson and James, where it announces itself as "radical empiricism," and which is realized in a rather different way by Levinas and Deleuze. No matter how relevant the question concerning the possibilities for the condition of experience may be, it does not offer a steady anchor against the twists and turns of experience.

3

Response to the Alien

The question concerning the kind of experience in which the alien comes to appear is inseparably linked to the further question of how we meet this alien. This question is reflected in the motif of responsivity which is not conceivable without an ethical dimension. A responsive ethics which is guided by this motif, however, goes deeper than a philosophy of morals which from the beginning relies on commandments, rights, or values. The alien call is not indifferent, unlike a fact which does not concern us; however, this does not mean that it is subject to definite standards of validity. Rather, without an element of amorality, every morality sinks down into the herd morality.

1. Responsivity

A phenomenon like the alien, which shows itself only by eluding us, could be characterized as a *hyperphenomenon*. Accordingly, Husserl characterizes the alien as "a verifiable accessibility of what is inaccessible originally" (*Hua* I:144), and in one of his volumes, *On the Phenomenology of Intersubjectivity* (*Hua* XV:631), he speaks in a similarly paradoxical fashion about the "accessibility in genuine inaccessibility, in the mode of incomprehensibility."[1] On the social level, one encounters the corresponding structure of "belonging in non-belonging": everybody who belongs to a family, people, caste, religious community, or culture never entirely belongs to it. Remoteness, distance, farness, as well as the moments of solitude and being-out-of-place to which phenomenologists often refer in their analyses of alien experience, do not mean a diminishing of this experience; rather, they belong to its essence. At the core of any phenomenology of the alien one finds the insight that an experience of the alien, as we have characterized it above, does not mean a deficit, just as our experience of what lies in the past or in the future is in no way deficient. The radical character of the alien does not mean that the alien is something entirely different from the own and the familiar; however, it does mean that it can neither be deduced from the own nor subsumed under the general. As something which withdraws, the alien is not only a hyperphenomenon, but also a primordial phenomenon, like the phenomenon of contrast (see *Hua* XI:138). For this very reason, each alien experience is located on the hither side of sense and rule, that is, measured against the sense *toward* which we understand something and ourselves, and measured against the rules *by* which we operate when treating somebody or something in this or that fashion. The common characteristics of *intentionality* and *regularity* on which the emergence of a common world depends are not replaced by *responsivity,* but are certainly surpassed by it. Responsivity designates "answerability," which precedes the responsibility for everything that we do and say.[2]

Here we see traces of a different phenomenology which is not confined to the realm of sense; its logos shows features of an originary heterology. The transgression of the sphere of an intentional or rule-governed sense takes place in responding to *an alien demand that does not have sense and does not follow rule,* but which interrupts the familiar formations of sense and rule, thus provoking the creation of new ones. *What* I say in response owes its meaning to the challenge *to which* I respond. The alien which appears to us as the call of the alien or the outlook from the alien loses its alienness if the *responsive difference* between that to which we respond and that to which we answer is replaced by an intentional or rule-guided sense process. The responsive difference disappears behind a *significative* or *hermeneutic difference* in which something is apprehended or understood as something, and it disappears behind a *regulative difference* in which something is treated according to a norm. The phenomenological, hermeneutic, or regulative "as" hides the experience of the alien when understanding and communication deny their responsive character.

The alien as alien requires a responsive form of phenomenology that begins with that which challenges us, calls upon us, or puts our own possibilities in question in an alienating, shocking, or amazing fashion before we enter into our own wanting-to-know and wanting-to-understand situation. The pathos of the alien surpasses its questionability. It is, however, not the case that we replace the traditional primacy of questioning, which occurs either as a question of fact directly corresponding to a desire for knowledge or as an intersubjective question which nevertheless indirectly leads us onto the same path. Mere reversals in general never lead very far because they remain tied to that which they reverse. What we need is a shift of weight and a new orientation which opens up new paths. We have struggled for quite a while to show that the circle of questioning and responding, which aims at a fulfillment of intentions and rules and the symmetrical equalizing distribution of question- and response-roles, is not self-evident. It then becomes obvious that the classic dialogue with which each traditional philosophy rises and falls already presupposes an asymmetry of call and response and a hiatus between being-called and responding.

In all speech that leaves the ground of what has already been said there lies a promise that cannot be fulfilled by the consensus of turn-taking and the conformity of regulated behavior. Hölderlin's often-cited "conversation that we are" arises from the remoteness of the alien whose call precedes all partnership.

2. Call and Response

In the call of the Other which breaks the purposive circle of intentionality as much as the regulative circle of communication, the alien emerges *in actu.* This kind of call or *Anspruch,* as I would say in German, means two things at once: an appeal that is directed *at someone* and a claim or pretension *to something.* Peculiar to the call of the Other is the fact that both forms of *Anspruch,* i.e., appeal and claim, are intertwined. In the call that I receive, there is something that is demanded from me. This situationally embodied call precedes every moral or legal claim; the question of whether or not a claim is legitimate presupposes that it has already been received as a call. Here we reach the region *on the hither side of good and evil, right and wrong.*

Here morality shows us its blind spot. All attempts to found morality presuppose factual claims which are more than mere facts. The simple occurrence of someone asking me for directions or asking for my name becomes a fact only when it is treated as a fact which may happen along the lines of observing, stating, or recounting how someone asked me about something. But something which *becomes* a fact *is not* a fact. The factualization of the alien question cannot prevent me from being called by the question. Besides, responding does not begin with talking about something; it does not begin with talking at all, but instead with a looking-at and a listening-to which to some extent is inevitable. I cannot hear the imperative "Listen!" without listening to it. The command "Do not listen to me!" leads to the famous double bind: regardless of how one reacts, one always does it in the wrong way. Even attempting not to listen [*Weghören*] presupposes a certain listening, and attempting not to look [*Wegsehen*] presupposes a certain looking, just as Nietzsche's disrespect includes a certain respect.

The kind of responding which corresponds to the twofold demand likewise takes on a twofold form. The claim upon something corresponds to the answer I give. In terms of speech-act theory this has to do with the suitable *answer content* which is going to fill in the blank in the propositional content of questions or requests. Such an answer remedies a lack. But the very event of responding is in no way exhausted by this. The appeal directed to me corresponds to a *response* that fills no hole, but comes to *meet the invites and calls of the Other.* Responding in its full sense does not give what it has, but rather what it invents in responding.

Giving or refusing a response occurs on the level of the speech event, not at the level of the speech content. Giving an answer is not exhausted by the answer given in a way similar to how the denial distinguishes itself from negative propositions and how the desire for knowledge distinguishes itself from ignorance. The given answer might be taken over by an answering machine that reacts appropriately to a suitable inquiry. This would not hold for giving an answer, except in the case of a prefabricated dialogue where answers are simply triggered or called up like data. A machine that stops working is, however, not refusing to offer its service. Take, in contrast, Bartleby from Melville's story of the same name. With his stereotypical repetition "I would prefer not to," this scribe not only turns down the service which he must perform, but he brings his refusal to the extreme by not responding and terminating all communication. He is, as we would put it, unreceptive to courtesy, lavished on him by his employer, a philanthropically minded lawyer. The refusal to respond, the evasive formula of which pushes onto the margins of silence, points to the abysses of discourse which no factual dissent can capture. Responding is thus more than a sense-directed or rule-guided behavior. An additional indication of the doubling of the response into a response event and a response content lies in the fact that I can respond to a question with a counter-question, i.e., with a response which is not an answer in the sense of furnishing the information that another person is asking for. *Keine Antwort ist auch eine Antwort,* as we say in German, or in English: no answer is also an answer.

Responding that comes to meet the alien call is not restricted to spoken utterances. During the fulfillment of a request, the alien speech and my action often dovetail with each other; for example, when I do what I am asked to do. Furthermore, one can provoke a response with a glance and reply to a glance. Intersecting gazes are part of everyday life in large cities. Responding embodies an ethos of the senses that extends from greeting rituals down to lovers' playing. In the end, the ancient definition "The human being is an animal which has speech or reason" can be reformulated as follows: "The human being is an animal which responds." Consequently, the difference between human and animal, as well as that between human and machine, must be reconsidered.

3. Aspects of a Response Logic

Responsivity as a main feature of human behavior calls for a special *response logic* that differs considerably from the logic of intentional acts, from the logic of comprehension, or from the logic of communicative action. It leads to a corresponding form of rationality, namely a rationality which arises from responsivity itself.[3] In what follows, I would like to sketch four aspects of this peculiar logic, and simultaneously I want to show how traditional themes begin to shimmer in the light of responding.

(1) The call of the Other, which is more than a part of a whole or a case of law, obtains a specific form of *singularity*. This singularity indeed appears in the plural, but in such a way that it eludes the distinction between the particular and the universal. Such a singularity does not mean that something occurs only once, such as for instance a sound or a crime. Also, singularity does not just mean that something is classified as one case among others. We are not dealing with an individuality that, according to an ancient doctrine, is unsayable because it appears on the inferior margin of an all-covering universality. Rather, we deal with a singularity of events that appears as such when deviating from familiar events and inaugurating another way of seeing, thinking, and acting. In the life of individuals, as well as in the life of peoples and cultures, there are key events [*Schlüsselereignisse*] "which one does not forget" because they introduce symbolic orders, establish meanings, instigate histories, provoke responses, and create new obligations. In this regard the French Revolution was, at least for participating Europeans, not just one revolution among others, and from this uniqueness it becomes a kernel of crystallization for various myths and rites. Only when considered through the eyes of a third party does the French Revolution appear next to the American, the Russian, or the Chinese revolution as one among others; just as a child, who, once it has grown up, learns to consider its mother as one woman among other women and its birthplace as one place among other places.

(2) Likewise, the Other's call rejects the disjunction between facts and norms, "is" and "ought," which has dominated the field of practical philosophy since Hume and Kant. The call that gives something to see, to hear, to think, to feel, appears with a sort of *inevitability*, a *ne-cessitudo* in its literal sense, which is not derived from universal laws but, as a practical necessity, belongs to the essential presuppositions of our social existence in the world. This inevitability means that I cannot not respond to the Other's call once it reaches me; just as, according to Paul Watzlawick, I cannot not communicate because not-responding would be but a sort of responding. The double negation that lies in the fact that I cannot not re-

spond is known from the determination of necessity practiced by modal logic. The proposition "it is necessary that p" can be translated with the help of the possibility operator M as "not M (not-p)." The double negation refers to the requirements which can be grasped only indirectly, namely, as the necessary conditions for certain experiences without a possibility of deriving them positively. Along similar lines, Kant spoke of a "fact of reason," Husserl of the "necessity of a fact" or of an "absolute fact," just like Sartre attributed to the cogito a *nécessité de fait.* In its radicality, the call of the Other resembles traditional examples, such as striving for happiness, the drive for self-preservation, the categorical imperative, and human freedom, all of which—if they exist—are not a matter of our choice; they are beyond our need for justification. In Plato's view, it is not in our hands to strive for happiness, just as for Kant it is not up to our discretion whether we hear the voice of the moral law or not.

That from which our discourse and speech begin, and have always begun, cannot be observed, judged, or managed as something before our eyes or in our hands. It comes to light only *when* we say or do something. It is dependent on an indirect manner of speaking and communicating which is and remains connected to silence. This also holds true for the pull that emanates from the alien in general and especially from an alien culture. Certainly, there are learning processes that take place between cultures once the stage of an "intercultural dialogue" has been reached. One has as little control over this pull, however, as one has over wonder, or the mania of love. With disturbances of this kind, there is only the possibility of either yielding to them or evading them; they cannot be eliminated, just like the air we breathe.

(3) We have already seen in the previous chapter that singular events not only yield an inescapable call, they also provoke an unreachable deferment [*Nachträglichkeit*]. The response logic is inconceivable without that kind of temporality which we have earlier designated as *diastasis.* The genuine deferment of the response undermines the primacy of some original presence. The presence is not nothing—as a good many postmodern annihilators believe—but it is not self-sufficient. Responding takes place here and now, but it begins elsewhere. According to Derrida, this deferment leads to the fact that the original appears only "by a replacement," that is, supported by supplements that pull an endless chain of "originary repetitions" with them. The same deferment has to be attributed to those traumatic accidents that are only graspable in their aftereffects, as in the Wolf Man's childhood story presented by Freud. If one were to speak of a mere communicative distortion, one would be playing down the importance of what is at stake here. One would be overlooking the fact that the establishment of a communica-

tive field does not itself take place by a communicative agreement, just as the Basic Law of a country is not adopted in conformity with itself and complying with it is not integrated into the sections of the Constitution. The foundation of an order is an event that does not function as part of the order it makes possible. In this respect, each birth which opens a new world is something of a rebirth, since it is only comprehensible in retrospect. Thus freedom does not mean the ability to begin absolutely with oneself; rather, it means that I begin somewhere else. Whoever believes that he is to be able to begin with himself only repeats what already exists; this means exactly not to begin. Responding means to renounce a first and, consequently, also a last word.

(4) Going hand in hand with the temporal deferment of demand and response is a non-eliminable *asymmetry* that throws out of balance the traditional dialogue orientated toward common goals and following common rules, and it also leaves behind moral demands for equality such as those found in the Golden Rule. As Levinas shows, this asymmetry does not depend upon the fact that in an ongoing dialogue rules are distributed unequally; rather, the asymmetry depends upon the fact that call and response do not converge. Between question and answer there is just as little consensus as between request and fulfillment. The two clash in the same manner as two intersecting glances.

Meeting the call of the alien and giving the gift of an answer turn into mutual giving and taking only when the own and the alien are considered by a third party who draws comparisons and in the case of a conflict creates a balance. The viewpoint of the third party, which guarantees law and justice, is in a certain manner indispensable. Insofar as in discourse and action forms are repeated and rules or laws are applied, there is always some third person or instance in play. By subjecting the call of the alien to a universal law and thus by *equalizing what is unequal*, however, justice always contains an element of injustice. The attempt to produce a definitive symmetry between the own and the alien, and to make both equal to each other, would in the end be similar to the attempt to balance present and past, waking and sleeping, or life and death, as if one could at will cross the threshold that separates one from the other in either direction. But the alien does not allow this; it behaves like ideas that occur to us, like obsessions that haunt us, like dreams from which we never fully wake up. It originates from an irrevocable "once upon a time" and from an irrevocable "elsewhere."

If we detach responding from the given sense and the existent rules, we will need to distinguish between primarily *repetitive* or *reproductive* and primarily *innovative* or *productive* responding. Ordinary, normal responding has meaning and follows specific rules. Yet this does not hold for responding to unanticipated calls, which breaks through an existent order and changes the conditions for understanding and communication. But whenever and wherever the order of things and words is shaken, there opens a gap between the alien provocation we come to face and our own production. Here we run into the paradox of creative response which resembles Merleau-Ponty's paradox of creative expression.[4] The response is creative despite its being a response. The call does not belong to the order which integrates or subjects the response. Rather, the call only becomes a call *in the response* which it causes and precedes. Thus responding runs over a small ridge which separates bondage and compliance from arbitrariness and willfulness. The one who waits for ready-made responses does not have anything to say because everything has *already been said*. In turn, the one who speaks without responding does not have anything *to say* either because there is nothing for him to say. We invent what we respond, but not what we respond to and what gives weight to our speaking and acting.

4

Corporeal Experience Between Selfhood and Otherness

Corporeality and alienness are intimately connected. Alienness presents itself in the flesh, as absence in flesh and bone (*absence en chair et en os*) in the formulation of Sartre, which alludes to Husserl's presence in the flesh [*leibhaftige Gegenwart*] of the perceived object. In turn, a corporeal being is never entirely present to itself. The enigma of alienness is thus exacerbated in the enigma of the body, so that we again get entangled in the Cartesian and post-Cartesian adventures of modernity.

1. The Enigma of the Body

The destiny of the modern era is marked deeply by the fact that the mathematization of nature and the supremacy of the ego arise together and reinforce each other. In this simultaneity, everything that pertains to our bodily existence is twice overshadowed, once by the subject's autonomy and again by nature's measure. There is no better evidence for this process than Descartes' thought. Here it is the thinking ego that relates to things. In some of these things I recognize myself as a *res cogitans*. Some others appear as Others who think as I do, but most of them are merely physical examples of *res extensa*. But there remains the problem of justifying that a certain physical body stands out as my own body (*corpus meum*), proving there are other bodies animated by other minds. It is the irony of history that our body is simultaneously covered and discovered. Our bodies appear split off from ourselves, although they also belong to us to a certain extent, especially when they make us suffer.

Cartesian dualism is undermined by a first revision, which brings in sense experience and linguistic expressions. Admittedly it is indeed I who refers to things, to myself, and to others, but I do so only by means of my body, which is constantly intervening. No manipulation is possible without me using my hands, no communication can occur without my mouth and ears, there is no feeling without blood pressure and heartbeat and so on. But this process of concretization stops halfway. It is still presupposed that there is somebody or something that is incorporated and embodied without itself being a body through and through. Hence, there is a way out. So in the end, owing to the all-pervasive Spirit, why should I be prohibited from returning to myself and simultaneously reaching the totality of beings by internalizing what initially belonged to the exteriority of the body? In this way, I start from my limited self, and I end with an all-encompassing whole. It is not easy to say who departs further from the truth of the body, Descartes who takes the dualistic position, insisting on a gap between mind and body, or Hegel who, despite all dissipation, takes the monistic position, integrating the body into the totality of Spirit. Traces of these old debates reverberate today even in the domain of the human and life sciences. On the one hand, even neurophysiology insists on the distinction between first- and third-person perspectives. However, the utility of this distinction at the methodological and experimental levels notwithstanding, the question remains open as to how to determine the ominous X that is supposed to appear under the two different perspectives. On the other hand, in itself, every kind of monism, whether physical or biological, finds trouble when confronted with beings that are not only spoken about or seen by us, but for their own part also speak to us and look at us.

However, there is another kind of revision which reaches deeper than this Cartesian or semi-Cartesian trouble. Is it not rather that in a certain sense I *am* my body and you *are* your body, as some phenomenologists claim? Do I only *have* pains or perceptions as if I were the owner of my experience? If we assume, as Helmuth Plessner does, that being-a-body and having-a-body are closely connected, we are faced with a difference that pertains to the sphere of our body, constituting its very being rather than undermining it. Our bodily experience would then by far exceed the experience of the body. The experience of our body would presuppose the corporeality of experience similar to the way our experience of time presupposes the temporality of experience, as conceived by Husserl. Nietzsche, a forerunner of the phenomenology of the body, extolled the body as "great reason" or as a self which governs it as a "mighty sovereign" and an "unknown wise man" (Nietzsche 1980, 39–40). But if we pursue this vision any further, we may end up in the labyrinth of the body only to discover how the power of this sovereign affects the different members of the body and how the unknown wisdom of the body works. It is in the *Philosophie am Leitfaden des Leibes* envisioned by Nietzsche that the old words "object," "subject," "intersubjectivity," logos, and pathos are presented in a new way. In what follows, I would like to pursue just this vision, leaning on three key phenomenological themes—intentionality, self-awareness, and intersubjectivity—to show

how the traditional language of consciousness turns into a new language of bodily experience.

2. Sense and Affection

Earlier, when we discussed the general realm of sense, we designated intentionality as the shibboleth of phenomenology in the same manner Freud posed unconsciousness as the shibboleth of psychoanalysis. But in both cases, the key word is far from being the final word. It does not solve the enigma; instead, it opens a way onto an immense field of questions. If we assume that something is always given as something, i.e., is grasped, understood, or interpreted in a certain sense and in a definite way, then the question will be: How does the body figure in all this?

Certainly, our body participates in the work of experience in many ways, but it does not seem to author all the intentional acts ascribed to consciousness, including the consciousness of our body. It was Plato who was the first to insist that it is not our eyes that see, but rather our soul that sees by means of the eyes. However, the choice between the soul and the eyes may prove to be a false alternative. Let us turn again to the formula of something as something. What about the something which is taken as something? Initially, Husserl makes use of Aristotelian terms, speaking of a certain hyle, i.e., something out of which something is formed by intentional acts. This may be true on a level of normality where things are what they are and are known as such. Here we may distinguish the repeatable form from various materials by which it is realized, just as Aristotle does when referring to tables or houses and their materials. But things look rather different when we get to the roots of those experiences where things only become what they are going to be. Let us take the case of perception. Perceiving does not start with an act of observation; on the contrary, it arises with an event of attention that is aroused and provoked by what strikes me. Or take actions, for another example. They emerge from the situations marked as something that attracts or repulses, which frightens or tempts us. Our actions are, as Husserl already concedes, more staged than made (see *Hua* IV: 98, 259, 336). Actions run through phases of hesitation and rehearsal before they acquire a distinct shape. Memory functions in a similar way. As Nietzsche demonstrates in his *Genealogy of Morals*, we keep in mind only what hurts us, and our spontaneous memory, meticulously described by Bergson and Proust, follows our desires and not our will. We are again and again overcome by our past before the process of explicit presentification [*Vergegenwärtigung*] takes place. Finally, even our thinking starts from ideas which occur to us, from what in German is called *Einfälle*, rendered by Lacan as *incidences*. Obsessions and delusions are not merely distortions of a free thought that would be its own master.

The pathic undergrounds and backgrounds of experience, which were discussed in detail earlier, acquire both color and weight only if the bodily components of our sense-experience are considered without transforming them into a faded replica of mental acts and dispositions. Everything that appears as something has to be described not simply as something which receives or possesses its sense, but as something which provokes sense without being already meaningful in itself, i.e., as something by which we are touched, affected, stimulated, surprised, and somehow violated. I call this happening pathos, *Widerfahrnis*, or af-fect, marked by a hyphen in order to suggest that something is done to us which we do not initiate. In German the prefix *an-* allows for a series of verbs such as *Angehen, Anblicken, Anreden*, or *Antun*, and the later Husserl follows these linguistic markers when developing his theory of affection (see Zahavi 1999, chap. 7). One may ask if he goes far enough along this path to draw proper implications. In any case, behind intentional acts, ascribed to a subject in terms of authorship or origin, there appear events that overcome or happen to us. Those events belong neither to a first-person perspective as subjective acts that we perform, nor to the third-person perspective as an objective process registered or effected from the outside. They require a language in which the id or *Es* is entangled with me [*mich*] or tied to me [*mir*]. In this respect, the ego, appearing in the accusative or the dative, precedes the ego in the nominative. From the very beginning I am involved, but not under the title of a responsible author or agent. In order to underline this passive pre-status of the so-called subject I use the term "patient," which is to be taken in its literal sense. The corresponding status would be that of a respondent who re-sponds to what strikes him or her. The *Wodurch*, i.e., something that we are affected by, appears as such only in terms of a *Worauf*, i.e., of something to which we respond. The *Nachträglichkeit*, i.e., the posteriority of the response we are invited to give, corresponds to the *Vorgängigkeit*, i.e., the previousness of the pathos that overcomes us. So in everything we do we are separated from our own origin by a genuine delay of time. Without such a radical form of temporality, which connects what it separates and separates what it connects, the motive of passivity would lose its force. It would be either located inside as the subject's own limit, e.g., as the sign of its finitude, or outside as the brute remainder of reality, e.g., as uncoded stimulus.

At this point, the question of our body and its role has already been partly answered. Being affected by and exposed to what is alien to myself

[*Ichfremdes*] depends neither on our knowing nor on our willing, i.e., on our consciousness; it points back to our body. The domain of corporeality includes all that indubitably has to do with me yet without being done by me. In this regard, the body, which Merleau-Ponty in his *Phenomenology of Perception* called an "inborn complex" (Merleau-Ponty 1945, 99), comes close to the unconscious, to the "body ego" (*Körper-Ich*), and to the corporeal language of symptoms that we have inherited from Freud's psychoanalysis. But trying to cross the borderline between phenomenology and psychoanalysis is a far-reaching endeavor that many a phenomenologist has undertaken. In the context of this discussion, it may be sufficient to focus on what can be called the birth of sense out of pathos. Like any other sort of birth it comes by way of labor. All in all, our body seems to be more human than the mind that is merely in a functioning position. Therefore, we should not only ask the habitual question about what a computer can or cannot do, but rather query about what may or may not happen to it, what it responds to and does not respond to.

3. The Split Self

Whereas intentionality governs our exchange with the world, the search for self-consciousness or self-awareness brings us face-to-face with ourselves. Once more we are challenged by the question of how this self-reference appears when viewed from the standpoint of our body. In contrast to the earlier forms of self-reference like care for oneself evoked by both Heidegger and Foucault, the modern access to ourselves is largely assigned to so-called reflection. However, when put to use, this concept, which was borrowed from optics, creates treacherous pitfalls. Locke's attempt to take the self as something beside things, thus complementing an outer experience with an inner one, is doomed to fail once we engage in the sphere of intentionality. If I am somebody by whose intentional acts things are constituted as such and simultaneously somebody to whom they are given, the ego cannot be reduced to a mere "tag-end of the world" [*Endchen der Welt*] (*Hua* I:63). Thus, for Husserl, reflection does not mean a sort of inner experience, but transcendental reflection, i.e., the thematization of the correlation between meaning and act, including those horizons in which my living in the world unfolds. In other words, reflection transforms functioning intentionality into an explicit intentionality.

It is obvious that this reflection also displays many corporeal aspects. We see, hear, touch, and move ourselves. So our own corporeality "refers to itself" (*Hua* I:128). Every self-referential activity includes different forms of self-affection. When we look at ourselves in the mirror, hear our voice on the tape, or touch a sharp knife with our fingers, we surprise ourselves. We are captured by our own image, bewildered by our own voice, or we simply cut into our own flesh. But as long as we interpret this "being for oneself" as "being intentionally related to oneself" (*Hua* I:81), we become entangled in endless iteration. We flee from one reflection to the other without ever reaching what we are reflecting on. We may as well learn something important from this Sisyphean labor. Namely, that the bodily self is a non-thing [*Nicht-Ding*], which is never "bodily present" [*leibhaft gegenwärtig*], as things are. The chain of reflections hangs on a pre-reflective kernel of the living present which can only be grasped afterwards by a sort of "after-awareness" [*Nachgewahren*] (*Hua* VIII:89). Long-standing discussions revolving around self-consciousness have demonstrated *usque ad nauseam* that every attempt to constitute self-consciousness by reflection presupposes the self it is looking for. Even the so-called *auto-poiesis*, i.e., self-fabrication, if taken literally, cannot escape this dilemma.

But there are other problems that stand much closer to the issue of the body. Obviously, we are acquainted with numerous processes and states such as blood pressure, hormone balance, firing of neurons, and last but not least the functioning of "my brain," the central part of "my body." All of these pertain to my body without, however, participating in the above mentioned forms of sensory reflection. It makes no sense to declare that our brain reflects on itself as if it were the offspring of the ancient homunculus. When neurologists claim that the brain selects or evaluates certain stimuli, they are really referring to operations which do not need an operative self. Recursive processes, produced by operative loops, are rather different from ordinary reflective acts. It may be tempting to oppose this intrusion of physics into the sphere of our lived body by reducing the whole neurophysiological apparatus to a naturalistic attitude so that the so-called personalistic attitude remains intact. But we will not get rid of the soul–body problem by means of such a clear-cut distinction. Certainly, the brain as brain is a neurological construct, but not what we may call the "functioning brain," which announces itself in splitting headaches rather than merely in measurable data. The active brain belongs to our living body and is not some physical annex. The simple distinction between the two attitudes offered by Husserl is still too closely connected with the presumed consciousness of our body, and thus leads us back onto the Cartesian track. It sounds much more convincing when Husserl qualifies the body as the "transfer-point" [*Umschlagstelle*] between sense and natural causality (*Hua* IV:286). One such transfer we experience in everyday fatigue; as Paul Valery states in his *Cahiers I* (11:37): "Tiredness turns the 'body' into a strange thing" ("Par la fatigue le 'corps' devient chose étrangère"). My own body thus acquires the traits of an alien body. Furthermore, technology with its increasing number of techniques of the body brings about new problems calling forth a genuine form of phenomenotechnics. This can be shown by simple examples taken from our body's everyday life. When I hear my voice on a tape or see my face in a video I get into a situation where proximity and distance are entangled, and where all direct reflection is diverted by a peculiar form of deflection. Old photo albums in which I see myself as a child show who I was and who I could have been. A boy shows "hopes which were not yet his own; uncertain expectations of a desired honorable future which reached for him like the spread wings of a golden net," and so asks Ulrich, the "Man Without Qualities," what binder could be strong enough to keep us from splitting into pieces? (Musil 1978, 648).

These are real problems, and it may be tempting to leave them behind by taking refuge in a pure self, in a pure feeling of our body, in an immanence of life, in a sublime kind of self-affection which precedes all that pushes us outside ourselves: let it be the whirl of time, the ecstasies of intentionality, or the challenges posed by others. But such a bodily narcissism, as it can be found in Michel Henry or Hermann Schmitz, is based on untenable premises. To take the body as body always presupposes a certain distance to one's own body which Plessner calls "eccentric positionality." The pure body, or to put it in German, *Leib ohne Körper,* responds to the rule of Cartesianism: *sentio, ergo sum.* But becoming aware of what one feels and giving it some expression means more than merely submitting to one's feelings.

So we have to search for other ways. Insisting on a split self may be such a way. Once more Descartes will help us clarify what is at stake here. His position cannot be simply skipped, it has to be taken into account and transformed, or else it will return again and again like all the repressed matters do. According to the Cartesian view, there are two fundamental modes of being, thinking minds and extended things. To put the problem in terms of divergent ways of visibility, we can approach it as follows: minds are seeing, but cannot be seen, things are seen, but cannot see. By contrast, our body does not fit into this dualistic scheme. On the one hand, our body is exactly both at once: seeing and seen, hearing and heard, touching and touched, moving and moved. On the other hand, the one who sees and what is seen never coincide as it is presupposed in the case of *cogito* and *cogitatum.* This noncoincidence should be viewed as a liability, for it characterizes the very being of our body, which refers to itself and at the same time evades itself. The initial example of sensory reflection should not be treated as an aesthesiological version of the Aristotelian νόησις νοήσεως, with the end result being that a thinking of thinking turns into a seeing of seeing, an ὅρασις ὁράσεως as in Plotinus (*En.* 5.3.8). What escapes my own eyes is not the seen something or somebody, but the very event of becoming visible. Something strikes me and catches my eye. It is my own gaze which withdraws, and not my eyes as the sensory organs that I can indeed observe in the mirror and whose shapes or colors I can identify at any time. The gaze, which responds to what appears, has no color. To this extent it is invisible. When I note that my face in the mirror is reversed, I think of myself as me who is looking at myself from the mirror and not of myself as simply a reflection on a smooth surface, because in this case the reflection is in its proper place. If this self-withdrawal is compared to the blind spot on the retina, we must take care not to confuse the invisible reversal of the visible with a mere lacuna within the field of vision, as Ernst Mach reveals to us in a sketchy self-portrait.

Now, our body appears not only as visible, but also as audible, touchable, movable, expressive, and libidinous. The jagged lines of my own body spread out in different directions. Remember young Narcissus, who falls in love with his own mirror image and falls to his death. He is haunted by the nymph Echo, who only reacts and repeats what has been said, literally living off of hearsay. This twice-failed rendezvous, which Ovid presents to us in its mythical form, teaches us a lot about our bodily condition. The echo appears as an acoustic version of the looking-glass effect. We hear ourselves speaking although we are the ones who are speaking. Here we find the case of autoecholalia, where infants seek to imitate their own vocalizations, but also a special case of echolalia, namely, a repetition of what has been heard with which elderly people try to hamper their mental regression. Verbal hallucinations, in which patients hear voices as if from the outside, although they produce them by themselves, would be completely incomprehensible to us if we were to understand voice as what always entirely belongs to us. Cartesians should ask themselves how they could explain the fact that a thinking being is capable of hallucinating. Otherwise mental patients would be degraded to strange living beings, and psychiatry would lose, as has often been the case, its human face.

As for the moving body, it plays the role of *basso continuo* for all kinds of action. This is an old issue. In Aristotle's view, the body is moved by purposes which attract or repel our strivings. When detached from emotions reason moves nothing (see *Nic. Ethics* 6.2.1139a35-36). Motions and emotions go hand in hand. In modern times the movement of the body is also subjected to the dualistic perspective. In his treatise *Passiones animae*, Descartes draws a clear distinction between action, where I move something from the inside, and passion, where I am moved from the outside. Although he mentions interesting limit-cases, such as restlessness or unrest, these are not brought forth by objects, but are awakened (*Passiones animae* 2.51). The crucial alternative is the following: moving or being moved, or to put it in Kantian terms, causality of freedom or causality of nature. But if practical behavior as well as other forms of behavior start with being affected and continue by responding, we encounter the enigma of a creature that moves but not completely by itself. This creature would then participate and intervene in an ongoing motion which would also precede our initiative. Every player of a musical instrument knows that his or her fingers are swifter and more sensitive than any rational control could possibly be. And likewise, any soccer player knows that his feet think along when they follow the ball as if guided by the navigator who lives inside his body. We are carried away (*mitgerissen, comportés*) by our own words and actions as well as by those of others, so that we are neither reduced to merely moved objects nor to simply moving subjects. That is why our everyday life is infiltrated by what Freud calls *Fehlleistungen,* by a sort of parapraxis which belongs to our praxis without being reducible to voluntary decisions. Being moved without moving and, vice versa, moving without being moved are merely limit-cases. In them we either descend to the lower state of lifeless things or ascend to the higher desireless state of the godlike "prime mover" who, according to Aristotle, moves by being loved (κινεῖ ὡς ἐρώμενον) without himself loving (Aristotle 1984, 1072b3).

We could continue in this way and show that all our behavior arises from a sort of self-affection we undergo as we respond to it. We are older than ourselves. As a result of our birth and a chain of rebirths, we are incapable of making up our *Selbstvorsprung,* our precedence to ourselves. The birth of sense out of pathos, mentioned above, is reinforced in the birth of myself out of pathos. My posteriority generates an irreducible sort of alienness which I call ecstatic alienness. I get outside of myself, not by chance, illness, or weakness, but by being who I am. This alterity results from a broken self-reference, i.e., a sort of self-reference which includes certain forms of self-withdrawal. Connected with myself and at the same time cut off from myself, I am neither simply one nor simply two, but two in one and one in two. The inner tension between both poles leaves room for extreme forms of fusion as well as dismemberment. Both monism and dualism find a certain truth here.

Concerning the old problem of the relationship between soul and body, we could speak of a *Leibkörper,* in a precise sense, as Husserl, Scheler, and Plessner did. This complex being includes not only the lived body by and through which we perceive and manipulate things, by which and through which we express ourselves and collaborate with each other; but it also includes all the physiological apparatus, with neurological and genetic processes, by which our own behavior is not only realized but to some extent shaped. All this belongs to us, but in terms of a decreasing proximity and an increasing distance. I am justified in speaking of a certain brain as my brain. We must only take into consideration that belonging to me does not *eo ipso* mean being at my disposal, as if I were the owner of my body. We direct our eyes, we stretch out our hands, or we speed up our steps, but we do not hold our breath or increase our blood pressure as if we were adjusting a computer program. This does not exclude the fact that the so-called higher activities of thinking and willing interact in multiple ways with physiological processes. Strong affects such as wonder or anxiety, which break into our normal life and provoke reactions, are in general surrounded by a special aura of corporeality. This holds true for the θαυμάζειν in Plato's *Theaetetus* (155c), which comes with the experience of vertigo, which makes us lose direction and sends our body spinning. It also holds for *admiratio* in Descartes' *Passiones animae* (2.74), which provokes a paralysis turning the body into a statue, as it were. If we take care not to submit thinking and speaking exclusively to the standards of clearness or correctness, and if we accentuate deep convictions and long-lasting habits, nothing should prevent us from admitting of an incarnate form of thinking which in German can be rendered as *leibhaftig*. There is no thinking and willing without deep convictions and habits which are far from being at our free disposal. It took a novelist such as Dostoevsky to make the daring suggestion that in the dark of night we believe differently than in the light of day. And it was Nietzsche who accused the philosophers of growing their ideas from sitting [*ersessen*] rather than collecting them from walking [*ergangen*]. In German, we speak of *Gedankengänge*, or "trails of thought." We should take Gassendi's *ambulo ergo sum* not as the reversal of Descartes' *cogito ergo sum*, but as its embodiment.

The continuous scale of proximity and distance leaves room for the most diverse forms of pathology. Let me recall cases of depersonalization where the patient's hand lies on the table like a stone, cases of schizophrenia where somebody is cut off from his own ideas, or cases of trauma where somebody is fixated on what happened to him, unable to adequately respond to it. But such pathological fissures do not fall completely outside the normal splitting of our self, which is always pervaded and haunted by certain anomalies. An attempt to escape from chaos by way of excessive normalization may bring about similar pathologies. Con-

sidered from the standpoint of the body, illness calls for various thera-
peutic interventions aimed at overcoming the Cartesian division into so-
matic and mental disease. We should make other distinctions, e.g., the
distinction between forms of disease which remain on the periphery of
the bodily self and other forms which touch the heart of our existence.
When Pascal ascribed to the human being the paradoxical state of a
"thinking reed" he came closer to the truth of the body than Descartes,
who only subsequently, by turning from the order of reason to the order
of life, conceded to a mixture of soul and body.

4. The Other as My Double

The alienness within myself opens paths to the alienness of the Other. It
prevents us from stumbling back onto the paths of traditional dualism.
From this point of view, there are some bodies which are to be called
other bodies only in relationship to other minds.[1] Whenever I start from
a consciousness of the alien (*Fremdbewußtsein*), the alienness of the Other
will be inevitably constituted on the basis of my "sphere of ownness,"
"within and by means of that which is my own" (*Hua* I:131). The alienness of the Other will be forever derived from one's own. The Other
appears as an alter ego, i.e., strictly speaking, as a second I. But as soon
as we adopt the standpoint of the body and proceed from a bodily self
who is "not a master in his own house," the Other arises as co-original
with myself and to some extent as preceding myself. In order to avoid
the traditional egocentrism based on a *subjectum* underlying everything
and everybody we are confronted with, we should follow Merleau-Ponty,
who replaced the term "intersubjectivity" with "intercorporeality." The
change of the basic scheme also changes the nature of the in-between;
it changes the dia- or the inter- which recurs with nuanced variations in
dia-logue, in *entre-tien* or inter-course.

When we now consider the status of the Other we encounter two
aspects which prove to be particularly important. First, the Other originally appears neither as something—which I transform into somebody
by way of empathy or analogy—nor as somebody—whose intentions I
understand, interpret, or share. On the contrary, the otherness or the alienness of the Other announces itself in terms of pathos, as specific *Fremd-
affektion*. We are touched by others before being able to ask who they are
and what their expressions mean. The alienness of the Other overcomes
and surprises us, disturbing our intentions before being understood in
this or that sense. The second aspect I want to emphasize stems from

the fact that I am not only affected by another ego or subject, i.e., by somebody different from myself, but by *meinesgleichen*, by *mon semblable*, by my alike who are, at the same time, incomparable, *unvergleichlich, hors de série*. We should not take the entry of the Other for granted as do so many theorists of language, society, and culture. There is not only a "miracle of reason," evoked already by Leibniz and taken up later by Husserl and Merleau-Ponty, there is also a "miracle of the Other," in a sense that there is no sufficient reason capable of explaining this miracle. We have apples, tables, or computers, just like the one before my eyes or in my hands, but none of these things has something like itself for an equal. Being somebody rather than merely something implies having equals, but these equals remain unequal because of their singularity, which is rooted in their incarnate being, in their being here and now. I call this strange fact, which cannot be derived from anything else, the doubling of myself in and by the Other. In this way my own ecstatic alienness is reinforced by the duplicating alienness of the Other. Belonging to this context is the disturbing phenomenon of the double, the doppelgänger which has been connected to the existence of the Other exceptionally strongly by Paul Valéry. In his *Cahiers,* he writes: "The Other, another like me, or perhaps a double of mine, that is the most magnetic abyss—the most reviving question, the most malicious obstacle—something which alone prevents all that remains from being confused, from being altogether estranged. Ape more than imitator—reflex which responds, precedes, amazes" (Valéry 1973, 499).

This strange kind of alienness can be illustrated by the same examples we have already drawn upon when elucidating my own alienness. The alien gaze, to which I am exposed, consists in the fact that I feel myself being seen before seeing the Other as somebody who is seeing things, including myself. The fact that I feel myself seen reaches its extreme in a special form of paranoia of feeling as if being constantly observed [*Beobachtungswahn*]. It cannot be reduced to the simple effect, accepted as sufficient by system theorists, that I see what you do not see. The "blind spot," inherent in all alien experience, exceeds the mere limits of capacity attributed to self-referential systems that are unable to integrate their own functioning. It makes no sense to claim that a machine feels persecuted by the sensors of other machines. The human other not only confronts us with the limits of our own possibilities, the Other's affection overcomes us as *wirkende Wirklichkeit,* as affective reality preceding the conditions of possibility, analyzed by transcendental philosophy and specified in terms of normative systems or codes. The alien experience is strictly speaking impossible; it is not made possible in advance either by my own initiative or by general rules. Following Schelling, we may call it immemorial [*unvordenklich*].

What holds true for the alien gaze also characterizes the alien voice. If I feel I am being addressed, this feeling is not limited to hearing somebody uttering certain words or producing certain sounds. Being appealed to by somebody and listening to somebody is more than hearing something said or uttered by the Other. Many linguists and some linguistics-oriented philosophers forget that there is no mutual understanding and no intention without attention, i.e., without something becoming aroused or given as a gift and not at all produced or exchanged. What we call pathos or affection is marked by the features of alienness [*Ichfremdheit*] before we ascribe this affection to somebody who may have caused it. As we have seen, gaze and voice are not restricted to the event of becoming visible or audible; rather, they include myself as somebody who is being seen and addressed. This means that I perceive myself from elsewhere. All this belongs to everyday situations that have non-everydayness for their background; moreover, this condition is deeply anchored in our own genesis. This can be demonstrated by the process of naming. The so-called proper name is in actuality a half-alien name because it is given by others. The name by which I am called is mine because I respond to it, whereas an object is not expected to adopt its label. Furthermore, there are numerous habits and mannerisms incorporated into my social body. Even my own language comes from others, and that is why we call it our mother tongue. In general, we must admit that we literally know our own language from hearsay. Finally, our body is a gendered and sexed body, largely shaped by the desire of the Other. The latter has to be understood in a twofold way, as the desire that comes from the Other and the desire that goes toward the Other. Taking into account that the Other is implanted into us, as it were, from the child's early symbiosis with its mother, we may follow the psychoanalyst Jean Laplanche and claim primacy of the seductive other (Laplanche 1997). We cannot reach the Other qua Other without starting from him or her.

However, it does not follow that we should simply reverse the inherited egocentrism and replace it with allocentrism, for it is also true that we cannot start from the Other without referring implicitly to ourselves. Alien love does not go back to self-love; nor can it be thought without self-love. Moreover, similar to how my body as *Leibkörper* runs a continuous scale of proximity and distance, my social body belongs only more or less to myself, depending on a changing degree of proximity and distance in relation to others. Intercorporeality implies that the own and the alien are entangled, that everybody is inserted into a nexus, into a *Geflecht,* as both Norbert Elias and Merleau-Ponty assert. Here, with Merleau-Ponty, we can even speak of social syncretism (see *Antwortregister,* part III, chapter 8). There are no ready-made individuals; rather there are only processes of individuation, which subject our bodily selves to a certain degree of anonymity and endow them with corporeal typicality. What we feel, perceive, do, or say interweaves, like a Tibetan carpet, with what others feel, perceive, do, or say. What one [*Man*] does or says does not inevitably sink to the level of inauthenticity or vulgarity [*Uneigentlich-keit* or *Vulgarität*]; rather, it constitutes the general background of what we do or say in our own name. It only becomes inauthentic if an individual behaves in such a way as to identify with public opinion or conventional morality. And that is not all. Somebody who has received his or her name from others and therefore does not own it, unlike a birthmark, retains a namelessness in his or her innermost core. Ancient taboos of using names or making images point to an inviolability of ourselves that presupposes an alienness and remoteness of our body. Consequently, we must assume that our body functions as a "transfer-point" [*Umschlag-stelle*], and not only because doing and suffering, culture and nature, permeate each other, but also because one's own is transformed into the alien and vice versa. To speak of "my own body" or of a *corps propre* expresses only half the truth. In his theory of the novel Mikhail Bakhtin develops the idea of "inner dialogism" of speech. He claims that each word is a "half-alien word" because it is "charged, even overcharged by others' intentions" (Bakhtin 1979, 185). In a similar way, my own body could be described as a half-alien body, charged by alien intentions, but also desires, projections, habits, affections, and violations, coming from others.

In the end, our bodily and embodied experiences show that I have the Other within myself and myself within the Other before we encounter each other. As Merleau-Ponty emphasizes, others appear within myself and at my side before coming face-to-face with me. In *The Prose of the World* he writes, "The Other . . . is thus always on the margin of what I see and hear, he is this side of me, he is beside or behind me, but he is not in that place which my look flattens and empties of any 'interior.' . . . He is like that double which the sick man feels always at his side, who resembles him like a brother, upon whom he could never fix without making him disappear" (1969, 186; 1973, 134). And even when facing the Other I am not standing with him on the same level. Our exchange takes place on an inclined plane, and it is always the Other who occupies the upper part. The alien call comes from the "height," according to Levinas, since it transcends my own expectations, wishes, and ideas, and overcomes us before we are able to assume a proper position on it. However, we ought to be aware of misunderstandings. The sublimity of the Other, which is so much at stake here, characterizes the Other as a respective Other who cannot be separated from the here and now of a specific order. He must not be confused with a wholly other outside of any order, nor with a social other, who enjoys a higher status and is superior to myself due to his authority or power. The Other does not succeed to a throne or altar. Only if we understand "height" as social hierarchy, would we allow for a dubious alliance of elevating the alien and lowering the self to the point of crawling, as Kant rightfully condemned.

The asymmetry in question here (see p. 41) is a multivaried asymmetry, but this variety cannot be reconciled, according to the "eye for an eye" principle, as some general symmetry. Nor is the point that I should prefer alien interests to my own interests. Our bodily experience of the Other has nothing to do with the eighteenth-century altruism that is but a corrective counterpart to a taken-for-granted egoism. In the beginning, it is not I who does or does not prefer the Other; it is rather experience itself that pre-fers. Just as any affect surprises us, as long as it is not normalized and channeled, the others' affection overcomes us. Summing up our previous formulations we can say: The pathos which gives birth to sense and to myself, bears the features of an allopathos which begins from others. We will never be completely settled in our own body as if we owned ourselves; but, maybe, it is this very restlessness that keeps us living.

5

Thresholds of Attention

Attention is something so ordinary that it is rarely considered in connection with the problem of the alien. Consequently, we might be missing one of the most important ways in which the alien comes to meet us, because it is intrinsic for attention that the senses can be controlled only to a limited extent. If the controls were perfect, life would be determined only by habit without allowing for anything of the alien. What the phenomenology of attention brings to the fore is the same ambivalence that we find in the phenomenology of the alien. When something comes to a person's attention, at first he does not know with what or whom he is dealing. Attending itself is the first response to the alien. Coming-to-attention and attending-to complement each other in the same manner as the previously discussed duet of pathos and response.

1. Attending

Let us begin with attending-to, from which the word "attention" derives. Attending-to is an everyday occurrence which philosophy hesitates to tackle, just as it hesitates to tackle a number of other matters. Obviously, it does not suffice to say that there is a lamp standing in front of me on the table, or that the church bell rings every hour, or that a car suddenly screeches to a stop right in front of me, or that I bump into an old friend: I need to notice all this. Apparently, I need to add something else in order for objects, living beings, or fellow humans to become part of my experience, but what is it exactly that I add? The answer might be myself. How do I make this happen? Shall I use a searchlight or give myself a clue?

Suggestions like these make us think of a stage director whom modernity calls the "subject." Yet the subject's history is far more colorful than any official history can possibly be. There is a certain awkwardness in the way that old European languages express the phenomenon of attention. In Greek, one speaks of προσέχειν, *holding-toward* and *directing-toward*, like a ship sailing toward the shore; in the case of attention, however, it is not a ship which proceeds toward an object, but spirit:

προσέχειν τὸν νοῦν, as everyday usage has it (see Plato, *Republic* 376a9).
It is not altogether different in German when we look at *Zuwendung,*
or *turning-toward.* Attending-to is set in motion and continuously pulled
under by the allure of what is seen and heard. Concerned with the education of the senses when discussing the education of the city guardians,
Plato resists the idea that vision should be "injected" into the soul. The
soul already possesses the capacity for knowledge: it is just not "turned
the right way to look where it ought to look"; "a craft of turning around"
is needed (*Republic* 518d). This turning around presupposes that we
move in a field of vision where some things are visible, whereas others
are not. From the Romance languages we know the Latin word *attentio,*
which also involves the spirit or the soul, as in *attendere animum.* The Latin
version, developed in a philosophical and theological context by Augustine, points to a certain *tension* (Lat. *tensio*) in the play of forces between
the soul and the body. Attention arises from the focused tension which
must prevail against numerous distractions and diversions.

The tendency to control attention increases in the modern era, especially with Descartes. As an act of the will, attention is subjected to the
cogito; yet, although Descartes counters *attention* with the shock of *admi-
ration,* later on the passive component is assigned to blind mechanisms
more and more. As a result, attention joins the counterplay of subject
and object, of one's own acts and of alien influences, of spiritualization
and of naturalization, which continues to this day. At the same time,
beginning with Henri Bergson, William James, Edmund Husserl, and
Walter Benjamin, philosophy has assigned increased attention to its own
role; recent research in neurology points in this direction as well. There
are experiments which confirm that the orientation of attention influences elementary reactions of the sensory centers located in the brain
and cannot be considered simply as an additional "subjective factor."

2. With All Senses

We begin by offering a few samples of attention aimed at both convey-
ing the flavor of the matter and illustrating the relation of attention
to different senses. In order for the multiplicity of phenomena to receive their due, the philosopher is always well advised to draw on literary
examples.

Wine lovers. Plato would not be a true Greek if he were to advocate
a sober spirit; yet this does not mean that he is enamored of wine. When
in the *Republic* the Song of Songs of philosophy is being performed, we

encounter the wine lover (φίλοινος) sitting right next to the lover of boys who gets up to deliver some sort of Leporello aria. He resembles the lover of wisdom (φιλόσοφος) because, just like the philosopher, he is "insatiable" as far as any kind of knowledge is concerned, and so is the *oinosoph* who "loves every kind of wine and finds any excuse to enjoy it" (*Republic* 475a). At the same time, wine lovers are merely harbingers of philosophy. Similarly to the lovers of hearing (φιλήκοοι) and seeing (φιλοθεάμονες) who pursue beautiful sounds, colors, and shapes without being concerned with the nature of the beautiful as such, we must also assume that a dedicated wine lover would let wine "melt on his tongue" without transforming the sensual into a sense or the spoken into a speaking tongue. But we then need to ask ourselves whether such an all-encompassing attention harms itself. Is it not that every lover is partial because there is no love without a preference [*Vorliebe*]? It was left to Hegel to climb the grapevine all the way up to the Bacchian heights of spirit and trade the defective love of wisdom for pure wisdom. Should we not, however, mistrust anybody who pretends to speak the truth and nothing but the truth? Should not *lingua* retain its ambiguity? Can the "mystery of bread and wine" be sublated into the "mystery of flesh and blood" as in the "Religion of Art" in the *Phenomenology of Spirit*? Should transformation be equated with elevation? Then it should rather be said that "youth is drunkenness without wine."

Dog concert. Now we shall descend into the lower regions of the audible, following Cynic paths. Dogs are among Plato's favorite animals; he endows them with a philosophical import because they are willing to learn and capable of distinguishing the familiar from the unfamiliar, the home (οἰκεῖον) from the alien (ἀλλότριον), and thus the friend from the foe. The attention demanded from the house- and city-animals, who abandoned their wild ways a long time ago, develops as a result of successful domestication. Just like the guardians who are to be educated, the guardian dogs see and hear what they are supposed to see and hear. The young dog from Kafka's "Investigations of a Dog" is a different matter. The dog remembers how a "little discrepancy" in his early experience made it obvious to him that "something was not quite right from the very beginning." That day something "exceptional" attracts his attention, something unheard of in the literal sense. He describes this occurrence in the following words:

> ". . . I greeted the morning excitedly with confused sounds, and then—as if in response to my summons—from some dark corner seven dogs stepped forth into the light, producing a terrible clamor the like of which I had never heard before. If I had not clearly seen that they were

dogs, and that they brought this clamor with them, though I failed to understand how they produced it, I would have run away at once; but as it was I stayed. At that time I knew next to nothing of that creative musical gift with which the dog species is alone endowed; till then it had escaped my powers of observation, which were only just slowly beginning to develop; naturally music had surrounded me ever since infancy as an unquestionable and indispensable element of life, but nothing had impelled me to distinguish it from the rest of my experience; only by such hints as were suitable to a childish understanding had my elders tried to draw my attention to it; all the more surprising to me therefore, indeed positively devastating, were these seven great musicians" (*Shorter Works,* 1:151).

"Who was forcing them to do what they were doing here?" wonders the young listener, who witnesses this odd occurrence as a "stranger." He suspects that there is a law or a call from the outside that forces them to make music, and thus it is more than a mere striving in which the same grows beyond itself while also remaining with itself in some sense, finding itself in the Good (see Plato, *Symposium* 205d). Since he does not receive any satisfying responses from the musician and other people, he begins exploring by himself "what it is that nourishes the dogs." It is the birth of literature out of music that Kafka lets us hear. For the dying writer Bergotte in Proust's *Recherche,* it is the *petit pan de mur jaune* in Vermeer's *View of Delft* that compels him to write as if a strange law were speaking to him. With this we move to the scale of the visible.

Gazes at the beach. Mr. Palomar is aimlessly meandering on the beach when he stumbles into the prohibitive presence of nudity: the "naked bosom" of a female. His gaze lingers. He wants to do justice to this "partial object" and makes four attempts in this respect. First, he sends his *gaze into the void,* striving for the "civil respect for the invisible frontier that surrounds people." But he soon realizes that every gazing-away includes some gazing-toward, even if only out of the corner of one's eye, and so he becomes aware that the more he represses his desire to see, the stronger it becomes. He thus attempts a *fixed gaze,* directed at its object in a straightforward fashion, but even this does not satisfy him; this "impartial uniformity" which integrates all female attributes into the landscape runs the risk of bringing the Other down to the level of mere objects. Such a gaze lacks discretion. On his third try the benevolent voyeur opts for a *surveying gaze,* which circles its precarious object of vision with an unprejudiced matter-of-factness but, as soon as it reaches the object, hesitates, steps back, starts searching for an evasive as well as a protective distance, and finally moves on "as if nothing happened." It is very unfortunate that the disrespectful gaze from above does not appreciate the female bosom and thus again lacks the necessary respect. Finally, he resorts to the *encompassing gaze*, which embraces the entire world, as it were.

"Now his gaze, giving the landscape a fickle glance, will linger on the breast with special consideration [*riguardo*], but will quickly include it in an impulse of good will and gratitude for the whole, for the sun and the sky, for the bent pines and the dune and the beach and the rocks and the clouds and the seaweed, for the cosmos that rotates around those haloed cusps."

The beauty on the beach, however, does not have much patience with this reconciliatory cosmic gaze. To get rid of the bothersome spectator, she throws on a towel, "shrugging in irritation," which expresses all sorts of things but certainly does not offer reciprocity for the gaze. "The dead weight of an intolerant tradition prevents anyone's properly understanding the most enlightened intentions," Palomar bitterly concludes. Perhaps, however, the all-too-carefully observed woman suspects that the no-gaze can be sufficiently encompassing to incorporate the pur-view [*An-blick*] of the individual. In sum, the "inclusion of the Other" has to fail already on the level of the gaze. Calvino's imaginative variations on attention serve as a reminder that recognition, respect, and attention are closely linked—more so than cognitive and voluntaristic models of attention would wish us to believe.

Syntacties and olfacties. It is paleontologist André Leroi-Gourhan who, as he traverses the millennia, considers the possibility that not only visual and audio works could be enacted, but also "syntacties" and "olfacties": "paintings in smell, symphonies of touch, architectures of balanced vibrations, poems of salt or acid taste" (1993, 283). He recommends that these sense-spheres, which have been neglected by the official aesthetics, should at least be granted a place "in the subterranean regions of our aesthetic life" (ibid.). Philosophy has not given much consideration to scents; they are too close to the animal realm. Yet every so often a back door opens, as in Aristotle's treatment of self-control (*Nic. Ethics* 3.13). Aristotle alerts us to the fact that not all visual, audio, and olfactory impressions seduce us into following our lust in an uninhibited fashion. The person who enjoys the smell of apples, roses, and incense can hardly be viewed as capable of losing control of his enjoyment. The situation changes where the smell of perfume and food is concerned, "for this is the enjoyment of the unrestrained people because it reminds them of things which they desire." Self-control thus also serves as a kind of attention filter which insures that logos is not subordinated to pathos. The diffused character of scents makes control difficult.

3. Basic Features of Attention

Attention does not deserve to be treated merely as one phenomenon among others; it is a key phenomenon which discloses experience in a unique fashion. Some basic features will be named, identified, and liberated from the traditional schemas of thought.

(1) From the start, we face the problem of categorizing attention. Are we concerned with a subjective act of attention, such as the inner gaze which scrutinizes matters with the precision of spirit (*acies mentis*), or anonymous mechanisms of observation which we can, under certain circumstances, entrust even to a TV monitor? The everyday and all-too-everyday experience which is conveyed to us in and through the above samples looks and sounds differently. At first, attending presents itself as an occurrence in which we are involved, yet not as its creators or law-givers. Attention must stay awake, otherwise it falls asleep. Likewise, as with the processes of awakening and falling asleep, we transgress a threshold which separates the familiar from the alien, the visible from the invisible, the audible from the inaudible, the touchable from the untouchable. What occurs beyond the threshold, where I am not and where I cannot be without becoming an other, appears attractive, horrifying, stimulating. All perception begins with something coming to my attention, imposing itself on me, attracting or repelling me, affecting me. Gestalt theoreticians like Kurt Lewin and Wolfgang Köhler speak of how one is attracted by the general appeal of things. Our seeing begins with something out there to see, and our hearing with something out there to hear. The gerund constitutes the anonymous figuration prior to the imperatives like "See!" or "Hear!" Such forms as gerund, exclamation mark, and imperative are part of the grammar of attention located on the hither side of the level of true propositions and right decisions.

Even the so-called higher activities, such as thinking and wanting, also begin with insights. They continuously depend on the thoughts which come and go and on the right word, that reconciliatory gesture arriving at the right time. Authors like Lichtenberg, Nietzsche, Freud, and Lacan, who refer to "it thinks" or, like Calvino, "it writes," should not be accused of trying to subvert reason or deny the subject its existence. The phenomenon of attention forces on us the assumption that something occurs *between me and the objects, between me and others,* which has no one-sided origin in me. At the same time I cannot help but be involved in it, whether in the strong form of a heightened attention or in the weaker form of a diffused attention which we name dozing off or daydreaming. In the past the secondary school transcript had an evaluative category called "keenness" [*Fleiß*] which appeared next to that of "attention" [*Aufmerksamkeit*], making one think that everything important hinged on the good will and understanding of the pupil. Yet how do we assess the kind of attention that needs to be awakened first?

(2) Attention necessarily involves *selection.* Turning-toward and turning-away occur at the same time. When we give attention to something, we take it away from something else. It is not by chance that the "narrowness of consciousness" is one of the oldest features of attention. We thus need to distinguish between a *listening-to* and *looking-at* and a *seeing* and *hearing of something* (compare French *écouter* vs. *entendre* and *regarder* vs. *voir*). This does not mean that there is an unchanging amount of data from which certain contents are selected, whereas others remain unselected; rather, attention forms an "affective relief" (*Hua* XI:168; *ACPAS,* 216). Our experiential field is organized by way of center points, margins, and backgrounds. Attention cannot decide on the "that," "what," and "who" of experience, but it certainly can decide about the "*how.*" This is the sense in which Husserl talks of "attentional changes," which he admittedly still relates in a one-sided fashion to the focusing "mental regard" of the ego (*Hua* III:59; *Ideas I,* 65). The process of attention which features a mixture of presence and absence allows for shades and for more or less, in contrast to the yes and no of the sphere of judgment which always yields an either-or. The horizons of experience are determined by an ineradicable indeterminacy; they are "foggy," as Husserl puts it (*Hua* III:65/59). The work of reason which brings everything into the light of the *lumières* finds itself confronted with the shadows of experience.

Since attention concerns the "how," i.e., the modalities of experience rather than its potentially truthful contents, it holds a special relation to technology, whose main aims are those means and ways which in the long run developed into machines and media systems. Electronic screens are our everyday *apparatuses of attention* and contribute to the constitution of reality and not just to the transfer of meaning. Plato, who thought so much about the magic of the senses and the seductive power of sounds and images, does not forget *sense technology* either. The lovers of sight, who were mentioned above and who take pleasure in the illusionary play of the senses, are at the same time the lovers of *techne* (φιλότεχνοι). For Plato, they sacrifice the essence of things to the mere ways of their production (*Republic* 476a). He makes fun of those lovers of sound who never miss a Dionysiac celebration and who have "their ears under contract" at all times, so that they do not miss any chorus, any concert (475d). The secondhand hearing and seeing which have taken on such gigantic proportions in our age of telehearing and televiewing and are enhanced by various hearing and visual aids are, for Plato, always in conflict with the "things themselves," which are only accessible to the ears and eyes of the spirit itself. It is precisely the phenomenon of attention, however, which endows the modalization of experience with such importance, that brings about its technization. Here too we find that phenomenology and phenomenotechnology go hand in hand.

(3) Furthermore, there is a specific *time* and specific *space* for attending. What comes to our mind and to our attention comes toward us, and it comes from a definite direction by coming closer or moving further away. The centripetal arrival from elsewhere—which needs to be distinguished from the centrifugal future of our projections—corresponds to a hesitation, a waiting, which does not yet know what to expect. Attention experiences a continuous *delay;* it is a lived patience that allows itself to be surprised. It also allows us to savor a taste, dwell on a view, appreciate a thought and also a mood. Far from the habitual secondary attention which expects something that is not yet present, the originary attention waits for something which will never be fully there. It not only extends experience but also increases it. Monsieur Teste thus confesses: "souffrir, c'est donner à quelque chose une attention suprême." The fact that we can learn from suffering is a commonplace which is not to be confused with the masochistic lust for suffering. Suffering means that something occurs to us, tearing us out of the familiar. It is only too true that there are affective "preoccupations of attention" and that habits fixate our attention until it becomes somewhat habitual, even for a professional such as a bodyguard. There is nothing lost by this way of attending because if a surprise overpowers us all learning becomes impossible; even more so, it becomes a rule. An experience which seeks nothing but to be shocked cannot even be surprised by this very shock any more. The unexpected relies on the contrast with the familiar. This contrast brings about the tension (*tensio*) which permeates attention (*attentio*).

(4) Mr. Palomar's gazing exercises show how closely attention is connected to adoration, to respect, to *regard,* to watching-out, to *Andenken,* which resonates with the Dutch word *andaacht* (= attention). In German, the word *Andacht* moved into the religious domain, albeit not completely, as can be demonstrated by such expressions as "mit Andacht lauschen" (listening with regard). It is only appropriate, then, that the German word for "attention" [*Aufmerksamkeit*] designates an interper-

sonal virtue which corresponds to *gentilezza* or *cortesia*. Those who keep an eye on the Other cannot help but notice when there is something wrong with him, but also if he is somehow joyful. Attention cannot be replaced by some "attention machine" because it can be either given or denied, not just to our cohabitants but also to things. This giving and denying is itself already a response to what we encounter, including the threatening possibility of forcing an access on the Other. Any attention can easily become harassment. Curiosity or *curiositas*, which concerns itself with many things without being invited by them, has an ambivalent character; it is neither a virtue nor a vice, but belongs to the arena of the senses. This much is certain: there is an ethos of the senses, and attention is an essential part of it. The fact that our manifold theories of language, action, and discourse neglect attention so crucially is not only somewhat connected to the fact that they have taken so much distance from the sensual "bathos of experience." This lack is ever more serious because the kind of attention which is selective in giving and denying has explosive conflict-generating contents. Overseeing and overhearing the demands of the alien bring the Other into a position in which he does *not even have the right to be wrong*. The normative machinery of demands and claims runs on empty in such cases. Lack of attention, however, can also let sheltering niches emerge. For example, Plato recommends taking refuge under a wall during politically disturbed and troublesome times, just as we take shelter from dusty winds and rain showers in the winter (*Republic* 496d). This was once called "internal emigration." Nobody can fully escape the alien gaze, however, the alien intrusion and complicity; therefore, the field of attention remains a place of struggle and suffering.

(5) The tensely woven field of attention also casts pathological shadows. Already in Augustine we encounter the polarity of collection and distraction, of concentration and dispersion, and the preference is often given to collection. Collection is more closely related to a spirit, which always returns to itself and to its origin and which unites everything in itself, rather than to the multiplicity and busyness of the senses. This relation proves questionable, however. From a pathological perspective, both exist: *over-concentration*, which becomes manifest in fixed ideas, and *over-distraction*, which finds expression in a flurry of ideas. Spatial anxieties like *agoraphobia* and *claustrophobia* touch upon and polarize attention. The person who avoids large open spaces or crowds feels overexposed to alien influences and gazes; the person who rather avoids closed spaces suffers from the narrowness of a situation which can be described as encapsulation. Once it occurs, attention becomes either diluted or solidified; in any case, it loses its hold or its horizon. There is something,

however, which escapes such polarizations, namely, the alien which awakens my attention or just my curiosity, but which also brings about a *disturbance of attention*. Freud points out repeatedly that the usual weakness of concentration does not sufficiently explain such errors as an oversight or a slip of the tongue because they show a play of forces which escapes both our knowing and our desiring. The split between the own and the alien which becomes manifest in profound and certainly not only pathological disturbances constitutes a threshold which can be transgressed by attention but never overcome by it. The pathologies then appear in a different light, namely as *clinging to the common, familiar, homey*, or as *fleeing into the extraordinary, exotic, excessive*. The opposite attempts to take hold on the hither side of the threshold or beyond it would fail, but in their own ways. Attention remains an unstable occurrence which can be neither fully normalized nor fully abnormalized.

4. Arts of Attention

Thresholds of attention play a special role in the audio and visual arts. This role is apparent when we consider gaze and sound. There are gazes which not only originate in the Other's eyes but also in the appearances of things and in the look which comes from a painting. There are sounds which are not only heard in the alien voice but also in musical tones and in the rustle of things. Gazes and sounds are never merely optical and acoustic phenomena, that is, *what is seen* and *what is heard* or what occurs in a world of vision and sound, but are also occurrences of *becoming visible* and *audible*.

Visual and audio arts can be regarded as laboratories of the senses in which the becoming of the visible and audible is thematized in itself. If we distinguish, with the art theoretician Max Imdahl, between a seeing that is seeing and a seeing that is being seen, between seeing differently and seeing again, and complement this duality with a hearing that is hearing and a hearing that is being heard, we encounter *the thresholds which separate the visible from the invisible, the audible from the inaudible*. In modern art, it is possible to encounter these thresholds in the extreme again and again. This holds, say, for Kasimir Malevich, whose black square resembles a background painting, a not-seeing-something which ends in a not-seeing. The painting no longer resembles a window through which we look out into the world; it becomes a black hole into which sinks the visible or from which it reemerges somewhat altered. In a different way, this holds for the musical attempts of John Cage when he makes us expect hearing by playing a silent piece or when he divides up a stream of sounds into sound drops which make room for individual sounds. Even apart from such extreme attempts, art which reaches its high point and does not sink down into conventional ways always performs a kind of *optical* or *acoustic epoché* which is not about refraining from judgment but rather deals with normal ways of seeing and hearing. Since the time of Plato, the motif of becoming blind and deaf has been a basic motif of the experience which abandons the solid ground of the familiar, and this is how the experience of thinking touches upon the experience of the arts. It presupposes, however, that the attentive kind of thinking, seeing, and hearing does not begin with itself but with something which touches our eyes and ears, af-fecting them, often unnoticed, by departing from the expected. Following Freud, we may assume that attention is at its most affective where it occurs not as directed, but as free-floating.

5. Techniques and Practices of Attention

Since attention, including its interruptions, is only conceivable on the basis of attitudes, it becomes realized as historically and culturally varied *techniques and practices of attention*. Exercises in seeing and hearing always involve an exercise in attending. An immense field of research has opened up here to which the American theoretician of art, Jonathan Crary, contributed rich material with his recent book *Suspensions of Perception*. In conclusion, however, I would merely like to point to two areas in which the diverse techniques and practices of attention become effective in specific ways: the economy and politics of attention.

The *economic* plays an elemental and inevitable role. The selection inherent in all attention, this simultaneity of turning-toward and turning-away, turns attention into a rare good which has by now also entered into the vortex of globalization. There are many providers who compete in the currently gigantic market of attention. Take, for example, the commercials which seek after attention in so many ways, using desirable images, erotic allusions, and intentional semantic leaps. The art of advertisement consists in setting a trap for our gaze. Advertisement artists are trappers. This is part and parcel of the gentle, furtive violence of economy. The *political* makes itself apparent because all attention takes place in a social space and can thus be more or less available for direction. There has always been a field of influence open to political or religious rhetoric, and for a long time it has defined the playing field of the intentional work of "public relations" and the ever-present mediality.

The politics of news reports is just one example. Every newspaper and every TV program decides randomly what is important and what should be filtered out, what becomes an object of speech and gaze and what does not. This filtering is not always as obvious as in the case of the news reports on the last Iraq war, which were indeed part of the warfare. The fact that intentionally wrong news was created, the so-called *dirty tricks* or *diversionary measures,* is not as important. The power is in the choice as such.

The political and the economic are also ingredients of attention. No fair redistribution of resources and no mutually consensual regulation can eliminate inevitable conflicts. Resistance is only to be expected from attention itself, in the shape of *attention sauvage,* an attention which preserves the moments of the an-economic and the anarchical and allows for a surplus of the given attention.

6

Between Cultures

What happens between cultures endows the alien with a special hue which leads to the development of a specific science of the alien—ethnology or cultural anthropology. The intercultural encounter has always been connected to a questionable form of colonial alien politics. Recently, ethnoscience and ethnopolitics have acquired new forms under the sign of globalization. However, this expanded perspective cannot deceive us about the fact that what happens between cultures always also reflects what happens between and to individuals. Not only does alienness start from ourselves, but the attempts to transgress it begin in our own home. The task of this chapter is to recapitulate the main episodes of the preceding considerations, albeit in an abbreviated shape.

1. Interculturality as In-Between Sphere

"Interculturality" should be taken literally. What happens between different cultures cannot be reduced to the simple fact that there are several cultures, all of which exhibit countable and comparable features or sets of features. Just as every comparison of language starts from a particular language, so does every comparison of culture. There is no place beyond cultures which could grant us an unbiased and unrestrained overview. As Europeans, we can escape our own culture just as little as we can our own body and our own language. There can be no culturalism which regards the own culture and the alien culture as one among others. Such a culturalism would simply repeat on the geographical-spatial plane what nineteenth-century historicism exercised on the historical-temporal plane. The museal culture, which Nietzsche denounced in his *Untimely Meditations,* would simply shift from the home to the exotic. The defects of multiculturalism only seem to be corrected when one tries to eliminate the boundaries that separate a specific culture, regardless if one understands individual cultures as parts of a universal culture, or if all these cultures are subjected to some transcultural standards. The "United Nations" is an institution which performs its duties in "a quick and dirty" fashion. To wait for the UN to turn into the "United Cultures" means procuring an intercultural Esperanto which has been long discarded as a linguistic utopia. We encounter something similar in the relation between the world market and world culture. Were we to trade ideas like we trade shares, they would soon become communicatively worn out; everything in them that provokes and unsettles would get lost. Nietzsche's "normal human" [*Normalmensch*] would have to find his dubitable home in the normal ideas of a normal culture.

However, if the word "interculturality" is taken seriously, we reach an in-between sphere not unlike Husserl's intersubjectivity or Merleau-Ponty's intercorporeality. Such an in-between sphere cannot, in its intermediary character, be reduced to something of its own or integrated into a whole; nor can it be submitted to universal laws. What happens between us belongs neither to each of us nor to all of us. It rather constitutes a no-man's land, a liminal landscape which simultaneously connects and separates. That which exists in such a way as to escape our access, we designate as alien. To be worthy of its name, interculturality must presume a division into own culture and alien culture; in the same vein Husserl assigns the alien-world to the home-world. Such a division does not exclude the processes of pluralization, universalization, or globalization; yet these processes would have to presuppose an experience of the alien which they never fulfill. The alien culture, just like one's own, is more than one culture among many, more than a partial culture or a playground for general laws. If this extra value is eliminated, we are doomed to step on the inclined plane of a unilateral absorption of the alien or an erasure of the difference between the own and the alien. Our Western history has been replete with such attempts.

2. The Ambiguity of the Alien

The problem of the alien begins with its name. Nothing is more common than the German word *fremd* (alien) and its variations and derivations like *Fremdling* (alien being), *Fremde* (alien land), *Fremdsprache* (alien language), *Fremdeln* (fear of the alien), *Entfremdung* (alienation), or *Verfremdung* (estrangement). However, as soon as we try to render the word *fremd* in other languages, we encounter a polysemy which exhibits three different nuances of meaning with the corresponding contrasts. *Fremd* is firstly that which occurs outside of one's own region as being exterior, in opposition to being *interior* (compare ξένον, *externum, extraneum, étranger,* stranger, foreigner). *Fremd* is secondly that which belongs to others (ἀλλότριον, *alienum,* alien, *ajeno*), in contrast to one's *own.* Belonging to this context is also the word *alienatio,* which is represented in the legal discourse as "severance," and clinically and sociopathologically as "withdrawal." Thirdly, *fremd* is that which belongs to a different kind, which is uncanny, peculiar, strange (ξένov, *insolitum, étrange*), in contrast to the *familiar.* The opposition exterior/interior points to a *place* of the alien, the opposition alien/own to *possession,* and the opposition strange/familiar to a *mode* of understanding. That these are different meanings becomes apparent as one and the same state of affairs can be alien in one sense, but not in another, like the house of the neighbor, which does not belong to me, but is very familiar, or a foreign colleague with whom I cooperate closely.

How shall we connect these different semantic variations? It is not a matter of mere homonymy. The "own" is obviously closer to the "interior" and "familiar" than to the "exterior" and "unfamiliar," with the connecting threads permeating all of these spheres. Rather, it might be the case of polysemy, which Aristotle attributes to beings and the Good. However, our next question is whether the different nuances of meaning operate on the same level or whether one of them runs supreme. Our reflections support the assumption that if we consider the experience of the radical alien, domineering will be the aspect of place. This fact becomes immediately obvious in that special way of drawing boundaries which allows for the emergence of something alien and not just something different.

3. Alienness Versus Otherness

We often speak of "otherness" when we mean "alienness." In other Western languages that do not have the rich semantic field provided by the German word *fremd,* the question of alienness is usually treated as the *question of the Other* or as *la question de l'Autre.* Yet for the most part, when speaking of otherness, we do not think of anything else but difference, and quite frequently, we allow ourselves to fall into a conceptual twilight that prevents the radical question of the alien from emerging. Furthermore, our Western traditions of thought assign a rather modest place to alienness; this happens not without reason but nevertheless has significant practical consequences.

Something is only the *same* if it distinguishes itself as *other* from others; this is one of the discoveries of Platonic dialectics, which had substantial speculative influence traveling through the centuries to Hegel. The contrast of the same and the other, on which every order of things is based, arises from a *division* that distinguishes one from the other. The result is a pervasive reversibility of positions: Asians are not Europeans, just like Europeans are not Asians. Moreover, this differentiation occurs in a common medium that mediates between the opposites. No matter how different Europeans and Asians are, they are undoubtedly human. It would be nice if every human being could speak in his or her own voice. However, intercultural experiences teach us only too well that behind such a voice there is always a specific authority speaking sotto voce for this human being without embodying him in all his universality. And all too often, there is a hierarchy hidden behind the pretense toward universality: Europeans speak about Europeans and non-Europeans, men about men and women, adults about adults and children, humans about humans and animals, those awake speak about the awake and also the sleeping. In all these cases, one side of the difference is clearly marked, but the other is not.

However, the difference between the own and the alien with which we are concerned here has as such nothing in common with the distinction between the same and the other. The Stranger from Elea, who enters the stage in the overture of Plato's *Sophist,* previewing the discussion about the dialectics of the same and the other, is not simply some other; like Zeus, who comes down from the heavens to inhabit human cities, the Stranger arrives from the other-land. The own is grouped around the *self,* as a bodily, ethnically, or culturally marked self. Even linguistically it is more or less distinctly separated from the same, as in Latin with the duality of *ipse* and *idem,* or in English with the duality of *self* and *same* (see p. 12). The jargon of identity, which has long overtaken the "jargon of authenticity," conceals simple states of affairs, like the one that I do not need to identify myself as bearer of pain in order to feel pain, or that somebody can feel threatened as a stranger without being able to name definitively his enemy, his stalker. The opposition between the own and the alien does not emerge from a mere separation, but from a process of *in-* and *ex-clusion.* I am where you cannot be, and vice versa. We call a place alien if it is where I am not and cannot be and where I am nevertheless, in the manner of this impossibility. We do not do justice to cultural differences if we compare them to different species of a plant- or animal-world where differences are sublated in a universal genus.[1] There is a threshold between the cultures, which is similar to those thresholds which separate one gender from the other, old age from youth, awakeness from sleep, and life from death (see p. 14). The ceremonial *rites de passages,* which, in archaic cultures, accompany transgressions of precarious thresholds, have not completely disappeared in our secular societies, although they have become more individualized and sometimes trivialized to the point of us no longer being capable of recognizing them. The separation between one experiential region and another must not be equated with the differentiation that comes about from the perspective of a mediating third. The thresholds that connect by separating do not allow for a mediator who could put a foot on both sides. The disjointing and, as a result, disjointed nature of the alien thus has nothing in common with the pure specification in which a universal becomes particular.

4. The Paradox of Alien Experience

When considering the most common determinations of alienness that even ethnology cannot do without, there are two that we encounter over and over again: that of the *inaccessibility* of a particular region of experience and sense, and that of *non-belonging* to a group. In the first case, *something* is alien to me or us; in the second, *others* are alien to me or us or vice versa. It is thus possible to distinguish between a *cultural* and a *social alienness;* yet, obviously, both determinations go hand in hand since culture presents itself as a social process, and socialization in turn is dependent on cultural symbolism. The experience that founds such in- and ex-clusion can, speaking with Husserl, be designated as alien experience [*Fremderfahrung*]. This experience certainly has a paradoxical character, which is also already announced by Husserl. We may speak of an accessibility of the inaccessible, a belonging in non-belonging, an incomprehensibility in the comprehensible (see p. 35). This does not mean that there is something in that experience that we cannot understand. Such an assumption would lead us straight into irrationalism. However, this also does not mean that we are dealing with something we are about to understand or no longer understand, moving within the horizon of our general comprehensibility. All these designations of the alien show a deficit. If there is a genuine alien experience which, just like the experience of time and space, is to be measured in itself and not against a potential omnipresence, then it does not constitute a surpassable lack. Rather, the alien experience means that absence and distance as "absence in the flesh" (Sartre), as "originary form of the elsewhere" (Merleau-Ponty), or as "non-place" of the alien face (Levinas), belong to the matter of the alien itself. Paradox here does not connote that the two designations of thought meet each other as antinomies; rather, it is one experience running counter to itself. Or we can call it a lived impossibility, which is implied by authors like Baudelaire, Valéry, Kafka, or Celan, but also already by Kierkegaard. The relation here presents itself as a form of withdrawal, as in the alien gaze that meets us before we know it, and from a distance that we cannot determine (as in an intimate touch, which does not mean that the distance between the touching and the touched is approaching zero but rather that we touch the ungraspable, the untouchable, as in the conversational pause without which there would never be an *entretien infini,* in the sense of Maurice Blanchot, and without which all our speech would remain caught in a monologue staged as dialogue).

By the term "radical" I designate an alienness that can neither be traced back to something of the own nor integrated into a whole, and which is therefore irreducible in the sense just explained. Such a radical alienness presupposes that the so-called subject is not a master of itself and that every order, which "there is" and which could always also be different, has its limits. Alienness in its radical form means that the self in a certain way lies *outside of itself* and that every order is surrounded by the shadows of the *extra-ordinary.* As long as we fail to see this insight, we are caught up in *relative* alienness, a mere alienness for us, which corresponds to a preliminary state of appropriation. This appropriation can occur in the political, religious, philosophical, or general cultural domains. It comes at the price of denying and violating the very alien experience from which every empowerment begins. Behind the often-quoted and formulaic "clash of civilizations," that which does not measure up to a thorough analysis might remain concealed. Certainly undeniable is the possibility of a return of the alien, of an alien which rises up against its appropriation, albeit on the wave of counter-violence.

5. The Nexus of Own and Alien

Alien experience does not connote that the own and the alien, the own body and the alien body, the mother tongue and the foreign language, the home culture and the alien culture are opposed to each other like monads, which are closed in themselves. The own, which originates equi-primordially with the alien and emerges as divided off from the alien, belongs to an in-between sphere which differentiates itself in different ways and to a different degree. In the beginning, there is neither the unity of a singular life form nor a plurality of personal and cultural life forms into which the unity merely multiplies itself; in other words, in the beginning, there is *difference.* Not only the attribute "alien," but also the attribute "own" has a relational character. Who would I be, and what would be my own if my ownness were not distinct from the other? The often-referenced solipsism is undermined by the fact that the *solus ipse* would not be a self because it would not be differentiated from anything or anybody. The one who insists on his ownness always reacts to a threat and by no means rests happily with himself. The "primordial distinction" between the own and the alien, which, despite all "transcendental solipsism," can also be found in Husserl as a process of differentiation, presupposes a certain indifference. It presupposes that the own and the alien, despite their separation, are more or less interwoven and entangled. This entanglement excludes a complete coinciding or melting of the own and the alien just as much as a complete disparity does. Therefore, we cannot speak of an absolutely or totally alien in either interpersonal or intercultural contexts. A language that is entirely alien to us could not even be conceived as an alien language. Just as some languages exhibit different forms of familiality, so do cultures. Here too we find both forms of elective affinity and forms of elective hostility. In the beginning, there is not just difference, but also a *mixture* that reveals every familial, national, racial, or cultural ideal of purity to be a mere phantasm. Furthermore, epochs and cultures differ from each other in the ways they treat the alien, i.e., in the ways they accept or reject it, incorporate it or let it be, and react toward it in a curious or self-sufficient way. There are different styles of alienness that cannot be brought to the common denominator. This is related to the fact that alienness, in contrast to otherness, exhibits an impregnable asymmetry, as our analyses of response logic and intercorporeality have shown. Whereas we can always reverse the formula "A is not B" into "B is not A," this does not hold for alien relations in the same way. Alien experiences exhibit a different shade that evades the differentiating language of pure identities and non-identities.

6. Alienness Within and Outside Ourselves

If the own is interwoven with the alien, this also means that the alien begins in ourselves and not outside ourselves, or rather, it means that we are never entirely at home with ourselves. I have been born into a world as an embodied being without ever being able to approach and appropriate the fact of my birth (see pp. 18, 41). I speak a language which I took over from others and literally know from hearsay. I bear a name which others have given to me and in which long-gone traditions reverberate. Again and again I reflect on myself in the gaze of the other. This *intrapersonal* alienness, which Rimbaud announces in "JE est un autre," takes on the traits of *intracultural* alienness. Our feelings and motivations, linguistic expressions, and cultural habits are not entirely accessible to any of us; nobody belongs fully to his culture. This could only be a lack if we assumed the existence of a completely self-transparent creature solely made of and by itself. Any discussion of one's own body, own language, or own culture needs to be taken *cum grano salis*. The grain of truth lies in the unavoidability and inescapability of the self, which is as such not a matter of choice. However, if we attribute to the self its features and ways as inherent characteristics, we enter the paths of materialist thought, whether on the personal or cultural level. Such materialist thinking is more developed in our modern Western culture than at other times and in other cultural regions. Anonymity is more prevalent in the Middle Ages than in the modern era; it carries more weight in traditional African cultures than in Western ones. There is a tendency toward individuation inherent in Western culture that can be summed up, with a certain satiric exaggeration, as follows: from the saint or wise man to the genius to the star. The "possessive individualism" which C. B. Macpherson attributes to the European modern era corresponds to a possessive culturalism which is equally one-sided and questionable and not at all suitable as a standard for transcending cultures.

Alien experience does not just mean that we encounter something alien; alien experience reaches its high point as our experience itself becomes alien. "Man is not a master in his own house"; otherwise, he could have kept the alien and the uncanny away from his body and escaped into his home. But the uncanny described by Freud well permeates the home; it does not dwell outside our own walls. As interpersonal alienness begins from intrapersonal alienness, so too does *intercultural* alienness begin from *intracultural* alienness. One could raise the following objection to this consideration: if there is no place in which an individual or a group is at home with itself, *chez soi*, then we are drowning in a sea of alienness; where everything is alien, in the end, nothing is alien any longer. Although this objection is noteworthy, it misses two points. My inaccessibility to myself surely includes an original proximity; without this proximity, the original distance of alienness would have no object. The fact that the own self can only be grasped from a distance does not mean that this self does not exist. Furthermore, internal and external alienness are not to be regarded as two parallel and separate forms of alienness, but rather as a double rhythm that realizes itself in one. I am alien to myself as I am haunted by the alien; I am also alien as I approach the alien, and respond to it. Someone who is astonished and startled by the alien is not his own master. Interpersonal or intercultural alienness cannot be separated from intrapersonal or intracultural alienness. But that is not all. It must be added that the alienness that we encounter in the other

leaves ever deeper traces in us the more it touches upon misplaced, repressed, and foregone matters of my own. As Merleau-Ponty writes in his
essay "From Mauss to Lévi-Strauss," there is a "wild region" that opens up
within one's own culture, yet is not enclosed in it. As a result, there opens
an access to alien cultures which—in line with Wittgenstein's remarks
about the *Golden Bough*—are more than just exotic curiosity or savvy cri-
tique in the style of Frazer.[2]

7. Collective Experience and Collective Speech

So far, we have treated interpersonal and intercultural experience in a
parallel fashion. Both the in-between character and the alien impulse are
indeed common to them. Yet our analysis must continue. What happens
when we encounter an alien culture or when civilizations clash? The social scientific perspective familiarizes us with the methodological distinction between individualism and holism. Individualism has come to replace larger social formations, such as a spirit of a people or a social class,
by introducing individual bearers of action to whom social and cultural
characteristics and attitudes are ascribed. Accordingly, there are no longer the German or the Polish peoples, but human beings who conceive
of themselves and behave as Germans or Poles and whose behavior is
rooted in their respective traditions and institutions. Social and cultural
belonging thus rests on habitually acquired or attributed features. But
the methodological distinction between individualism and holism by no
means does justice to the entanglement of the own and the alien.

From the perspective of the involved parties, a cultural exchange
can be expressed linguistically only by saying that "we" confront "you":
We the Germans—You the Polish, We the Europeans—You the Africans.
This collective confrontation does not need to happen on the level of
language; glances, gestures, or smells suffice for creating an alien sphere.
Yet let us remain with the explicit form of we-speech and you-address.
The "we" which is expressed in this collective exchange of words means
first and foremost an exclusive "we" that does not include the ones addressed; otherwise, alienness would from the beginning be sublated in
and through an encompassing commonality. Furthermore, "we" is not
to be understood as a simple plurality designating the multiplicity of
an "I" or "you," as when specific examples of a genus or elements of a
group are summarized. "We" belongs to the process of expression and
can never be entirely subsumed under the expressed content. Finally,

there is no "we" that says "we"; rather, it is me or someone else who says "we," meaning that an individual speaks for the others. The "we" needs a *spokesperson* who stands in for the group, even if this advocacy rotates and is not tied to one representative person or group of persons. Utterances containing expressions like "We the Germans" or "You the Africans" need to be examined regarding the place out of which somebody in this way speaks for others. Cultures meet each other either through outstanding or average representatives of their respective cultures. A gigantomachy of cultures, religions, or nations belongs to the domain of collective myths. Every speech that expresses an alien experience and does not take refuge in a pseudo-collective happens in a place that can never be fully integrated into the culture that is represented in it. In this respect, the place of speech resembles a place in which a map comes to be used; this place of usage can never be marked in the grid as just one place among others. The red dot on the map indicating the user's location points to a blind spot in our own field of vision and action. Similarly, the cultural "we" is related in an indexical fashion to a place in which it is always said anew. The we-talk belongs to those performative acts that do not just determine what is the case, but bring about certain effects. One of these effects is social belonging itself. In such we- and you-talk, the play between the own and alien cultures is brought to performance, including the distribution of leading and supporting roles, as well as the enforced in- and ex-clusion.

The relation of we-talk back to somebody who says "we" excludes that the lived and practiced interconnection of a group or culture becomes fixed to a collective entity. This prevents thinking in terms of totalities. Yet, conversely, this does not mean that we inevitably end up with the mere "community of individuals" that Norbert Elias problematizes so convincingly. The question "Who speaks, and from where?" certainly allows that the individual speaks only more or less in his own voice yet never exclusively in his own voice. The entanglement of the own and the alien in the intra- as well as inter-cultural realms not only permits it, but even demands it. As with Mikhail Bakhtin, we should assume a plurivocity inherent in each individual voice. We do not only encounter something alien when we speak about the alien; it already occurs implicitly in our own utterances, like citations which can never be fully explicated. The culture, which becomes vocal in speech but which is also embodied in the corporeal *habitus* and sedimented in sense formations, has its place in a corporeal and intercorporeal experience that is richer than all its possible explications. The body, which allows us to dwell in a world, not only serves as a "transfer point" between nature and spirit or between nature and culture; it also functions as a transfer point between the own and the alien, between the own and alien cultures. Therefore, we find the alien in the own and the own in the alien well before comparativists undertake their comparisons.

However, this entanglement of the own and the alien is not free from conflicts. This becomes obvious in an elementary fashion in the fact that the becoming of alien can take different directions. Are the others, the members of an alien community, an alien group, an alien culture *alien to us* or are *we alien to them*? The answer to this question depends on whether the own group serves as a point of reference or the alien group does. This inquiry is far from being a mute enterprise if we consider how much intercultural exchange has always been determined by waves of migration, by conquests, by deportation, that is, by transformations of home-worlds into alien-worlds and vice versa. Julia Kristeva's pronouncement "We are all aliens" (1988, 209) is as correct and trivial as the pronouncement "All languages are foreign languages." In addition to the fact that this generalization of occasional aliennesses does not eliminate alienness, it becomes obvious that one language can well be more alien than another. Alienness is not a general function which concerns all in turn; rather, it refers back to an experience which—as Kristeva herself sufficiently shows—is always also marked by insecurity, threat, and incomprehension. These very factors are distributed in an unequal fashion, depending on who determines the social and linguistic rules of the game, i.e., who "has the say." We are thus approaching the question of mediating powers that like to interfere in alien experience in a regulative fashion.

8. The Alien and the Third

The fact that the own and the alien are interwoven does not mean that both of them fit into an encompassing order or are even subject to a fundamental order. The alien call which draws us into the alien experience comes from elsewhere; there is something ex-territorial in it, which also means that it de-territorializes ourselves. The in-between sphere from which we began does not form a common ground on which alien experience could be possibly built; nor does it form a sovereign territory which would be submitted to a common law from the start. Alienness as inaccessibility and non-belonging ignites all attempts at mediation and appropriation. In the alien, I am both outside myself and outside of the specific existing orders. The interpenetration of the alien experience cannot be translated into an encompassing synthesis or a final contract.

However, both dispersal and intrusion of the alien presuppose the very orders that it interrupts. Inaccessibility and non-belonging refer to specific conditions of access and belonging, just like every anomaly is set apart from existent normalities. Alienness proves to be an *excess* which *exceeds* the respective pre-given senses and laws and *diverts* from them. In fact, it occurs solely in the shape of such excess and divergence. Every alien experience is and remains in this sense an experience of contrast that always involves the alien, albeit in an indirect fashion, and thus also requires an indirect way of speech and action. Before the alien arises as a theme, it makes itself known as disruption, interference, or disturbance, acquiring different affective shades of astonishment or anxiety. We should remember here the birth of philosophy out of wonder, in Plato, or out of anxiety, in Epicurus; but we should also remember the *fascinosum* and *tremendum* of religious conversion. Alienness can be circumscribed in many ways, and last but not least as a beginning which is not at all at our disposal. Every attempt at mastering the alien leads to a violent rationalization which attempts in vain to rid the self and rationality of their contingency and genesis. Alienness does not eliminate everything called "subject" and "rationality" following the language of our modern tradition; yet it yields the insight that nobody is ever entirely with himself or entirely at home in his world. This holds for personal experiences just as much as for cultural experiences in which our personal life finds its collective expression.

If we now contrast the figure of the alien to that of the third, we do not conceive of an individual added at random, thus increasing the number of group members; rather, we think of a specific role that is always assumed when we side with someone or go against the other. We cannot utter a word or carry out a gesture of action without a third coming into play, which can neither be reduced to the behavior of the addressee nor to that of the addresser. The third, no matter whether it is a personal or anonymous authority, stands in for rules, orders, and laws, therefore permitting us to address and treat something *as something*, somebody *as somebody*. This third, the traces of which we find in Simmel, Sartre, and Levinas, but also in Freud and Lacan (see Bedorf 2003), can take on different functions. Depending on the degree of involvement, we can distinguish between the *involved third* who intervenes in a process as an aid or a saboteur, e.g., by way of lauding or criticizing; the *witnessing third* who accounts for certain events, making them known or keeping them in mind; and the *neutrally observing third* who registers social processes without interfering or taking a position. The methodological debates of ethnology have been intensely concerned with these matters ever since they introduced a mixed form of the third as "participant observation."

When at war, we also make a distinction between those who fight and those who report about fighting, even though nowadays the boundaries are often blurred due to technological advances. Finally, the third can take on different functions of ordering, as *controller* who coordinates actions, as *distributor* who hands out rights or chances, as *mediator* who ends a conflict, or as *interpreter* who mediates between different forms of expression. No intercultural exchange is conceivable without such mediating accomplishments. In this context, it is certainly not insignificant which culture sends the respective mediator and which language of communication is used. Paraphrasing Marx, we may state that the dominant language is usually that of the dominating parties, even if it is restricted to an economic or cultural dominance. A biculturalism that would not depend on any mediation presents a limit case which never becomes realized in a pure form. Interpreters are no double-faced Januses.

The contamination of the alien with the third, as it becomes clear by this point, takes us to the actual problem, namely, the question as to how the figures of the alien and the third are related to each other. A configuration which would join the two figures into a unified one must be excluded, as our previous considerations have shown. Instead, we are confronted with a *multidimensionality* of experience. The crossing point between the axes of the alien and the third is situated where the alien in general and the alien being can be grasped *as* something and *as* somebody. In these ways of grasping, which are by necessity generalizing, there occurs an equation of the unequal, as Nietzsche notes in his elaborations in *On Truth and Lie in a Nonmoral Sense*. To be sure, the point is not to condemn this equating, as the defenders of a unified encompassing order or basic order like to do, blaming their adversaries. This equating is part of every ordering achievement which orders that which has never belonged to it. In this sense, there is a moment of injustice in every justice which has always consisted in treating the equal equally and the unequal unequally. This is a constitutive feature of every contingent order which proceeds in a selective and exclusive fashion. The aim cannot be to avoid such equating, but rather, to make apparent the genesis of orders and thus their inner contingency. This holds for both the cultural and intercultural realms: *there are orders, but there is no one order.*

A mingling of the above dimensions has dire consequences, and one of these consequences is the Eurocentrism that follows the European tradition like a shadow. The alien that evades a particular order has nothing in common with the specific that belongs to the applied field of general laws and norms. If the extra-ordinary status of the alien is adjusted to the intra-ordinary status of the specific, then the inevitable and justified standpoint *of the general* is transformed into a *general* standpoint under which everything is to be subsumed. In this case, we would enter the paths of universalization, which would not lose its questionable character even if it relies on big pronouncements like world reason, world culture, world bourgeoisie, world ethos, or humanity. The alternative to this hybrid universalism is not an ethnocentrism that falls back on the boundaries of one's own life form. Rather, the alternative is a transgression, a calling into question, a disturbance of the own by the alien, whose singular demands cannot be transferred into an encompassing or fundamental order. Alien is exactly that which cannot be "drawn in." A purely "inclusive community," as Jürgen Habermas envisions it, would be a community that denies its own boundaries, or it would be a mere construct of a community.[3] In any case, one would evade intercultural experience, which is inconceivable without alienness.

9. Xenology and Xenopolitics

Interculturality, which goes beyond exotic formative experiences and adventures, cannot be conceived without certain forms of alien science and alien politics. If ethnology (or cultural anthropology) is defined, with Karl-Heinz Kohl, as "a science of the cultural alien," then the question becomes what shape such a xenology might take.[4] If the alien were just one object among many which could be deciphered through specific methods of explanation and comprehension, then this science would be in a precarious position. In order to ensure an increasingly successful research, one would have to pay the price of a gradual diminishment of the self, for a comprehended and explained alien would lose its alien character. In the end, there would be no task left for a science of the alien. This paradox of an alien science turns into a fruitful paradox only when logos shows its own boundaries as also belonging to the alien. This would lead us to a form of *alogon* that is not just opposed to reason as something merely irrational (which would simply come down to an indirect confirmation), but that leaves its marks as moments of the "wild" in the logos of a culture. The ethnological experience from which any ethnological research departs constitutes its blind spot in the alienness of the alien culture. In addition, there is the fact that ethnology meanwhile has an ethnization of the neighboring sciences which can be compared to the mathematization of non-mathematical sciences. If there is an alienness inherent in logos itself, then it cannot be restricted to a special science of the alien.

Similar considerations hold for an ethnopolitics transcending the everyday practices and institutional measures of an alien politics. A politics that gives room to the alien would be characterized through the fact that there is an aspect of the apolitical inherent in the political (see p. 10). This apolitical must not be conflated with the unpolitical which would be located beyond the sphere of the political; rather, it must be understood as something which, within the realm of politics, evades the ordering grasp. Such an empty position within the polis, which resists any totalization and breaks open every inclusion, would have an eminent political effect. The political world order, no matter what it might look like, would remain porous.

10. Procedures of Estrangement

We continue to encounter the question of how we can deal with the alien without taking away its sting. The further question would be then, what can an intercultural exchange look like if it is to avoid a unilateral or general appropriation? We have already mentioned different motifs and procedures of estrangement, which break through the appropriative tendency. There is a special *atopia* of Socrates which allies with his whole philosophical existence; the *dépaysement* and *détachement* that Lévi-Strauss attributes to the ethnologist's initial experience and which he traces back to Rousseau; the productive *estrangement* which extends from the Russian Formalists[5] to Brecht and the Surrealists. As a phenomenologist, I propagate a specific kind of *epoché* that instigates a suspension of assumptions that are taken for granted, a departure from the familiar, a stepping-back in front of the alien. But is any of this sufficient? If the alien experience were something we could evoke purposefully and methodically, then the alien would again turn into a result stemming from our own measures and would fall subject to our own standards. The alien, which takes us outside ourselves and lets us transcend the boundaries of the specific order, cannot be anything that we bring about by our own volition. It is only conceivable as a pathos that happens to us. The ambiguity expressed in this word, which includes a suffering, saves us from a harmless interpretation of the alien. Only if we start elsewhere, in a place where we have never been and will never be, can we testify to such a happening, which is certainly not limited to intercultural experiences, yet develops a special virulence for them. I wish to designate speech that comes from an alien place as response. Responding to the alien means more than sense understanding and more than norm-guided communication, no matter how important all of these are. Intercultural experience cannot help but become weak interculturalism unless it—to speak with Celan—always again "goes through a pause."

Notes

Introduction

1. A formal outline of the phenomenology of the alien which I envision can be found in chapter 1 of *Topography of the Alien* (*Topographie des Fremden*, 1997). The different dimensions of the alien are examined in detail in chapters 5–6 of *The Jagged Lines of Experience* (*Bruchlinien der Erfahrung*, 2002).

2. In this instance, I deliberately diverge from the order in which these ideas were developed in order to facilitate the understanding, since *Response Register* presupposes some of that which is only fully unfolded in *The Jagged Lines*. The "to what" of responding points back to the "by what" of having been overcome.

3. Let me at this point mention the Vienna-based journal *Polylog, a Journal for Intercultural Philosophy*, in which by now quite a number of thematic issues have appeared.

4. This work draws upon the following earlier studies: Chapter 1: congress presentation in Düsseldorf, 1998, published in *Moderne(n) der Jahrhundert-wenden*, ed. V. Borsò and B. Goldammer (Baden-Baden: Nomos, 2000); Italian translation, Bologna 2003. Chapter 2: Jaspers lecture in Oldenburg and congress presentation in Bonn 2002; Italian translation published in *Paradigmi* 20, no. 60 (2002); Georgian translation, Tbilisi 2002; Chinese translation, Beijing 2004; German in *Grenzen und Grenzüberschreitungen* 19, German Congress for Philosophy, ed. W. Hogrebe (Berlin: Akademie, 2004). Chapter 3: published in *Der Anspruch des Anderen*, ed. B. Waldenfels and I. Därmann (Munich: Fink, 1998); first publication in Japanese, Osaka 1996; further publications in Spanish, Hungarian (1997), Russian, Czech (1998), Polish (1999), French (2000), Italian (2002), English and Georgian (2003). Chapter 4: lectures in Copenhagen 2002 and in Helsinki 2003, published in *Vernunft – Entwicklung – Leben*, ed. U. Bröckling, A. Paul, and St. Kaufmann (Munich: Fink, 2004); English translation in *Phenomenology and the Cognitive Sciences* 3 (2004); Finnish translation in *Ajatus* 61 (2004). Chapter 5: published in *Links* (Pisa, Rome) 2 (2002). Chapter 6: published in *Jahrbuch Deutsch als Fremdsprache*, ed. A. Wierlacher et al., vol. 26 (Munich: Iudicium, 2000); Italian translation in *Aut-Aut* no. 313–14 (2003).

Chapter 1

1. The figure of the *apolis* emerges from the background of the polis, and Sophocles contrasts it with the ὑψίπολις, the "outstanding one in the city'" (*Antigone* 5.370). The person who comes under the title of *apolis* corresponds to the "stateless person" in our current sense, but it can also be taken in a wider sense as analogous to the aforementioned *atopos* who is literally "placeless" and who is also considered to be "out of place" or "strange." The *alpha privativum* in both Greek expressions can be conceived not merely as a negation, but also as expressing a withdrawal.

2. See *Phänomenologie der Aufmerksamkeit,* chapter 3: "Unerzählbares."

3. See Vittoria Borsò, whose book *Mexiko jenseits der Einsamkeit—Versuch einer interkulturellen Analyse* (1994) contains an interesting view of the motif of the alien in contemporary literature and literary theory.

4. These ideas are explored in my *Grenzen der Normalisierung* (1998).

5. This impossibility is not limited to but includes a pathological side. See my contribution, "Gelebte Unmöglichkeit," in *Inszenierungen des Unmöglichen: Theorie und Therapie schwerer Persönlichkeitsstörungen,* ed. C. Rohde-Dachser and F. Wellendorf (2004).

Chapter 2

1. The aforementioned "as" is familiar to us from other languages as ᾗ, *qua, als, comme,* or *come.*

2. The old doctrine of catharsis would also need to be questioned again, no matter whether catharsis is conceived of as a cleansing of affects or a cleansing from affects. The process, understood half in medical, half in moral terms, which used to be called "cleansing" and is nowadays called "working through," turns all too easily into an affectively guided ordering of the pathic.

3. The fact that intentionality and causality are not separated by an abyss became clear to me early on (see *Der Spielraum des Verhaltens,* 1980, chapter 4). It just took some time to differentiate the concept of effect with sufficient precision.

4. We need, however, to note the growing significance of emotions both in psychology and in neurophysiology after they have long been in the shadow of cognitions which are more accessible to computer modeling. Hubert Dreyfus has brought phenomenological aspects into this debate for a long time, giving more credit to bodily situatedness, habitualization, and implicit knowledge than traditional role models.

5. See my reflections on the "aporias of violence" in Dabag, Kapust, Waldenfels 2000.

6. See the more detailed account in *Bruchlinien der Erfahrung,* chapter 8, 11-13.

Chapter 3

1. "Zugänglichkeit in der eigentlichen Unzugänglichkeit, im Modus der Unverständlichkeit."

2. I have borrowed the terms "responsivity" and "response" from the field of medicine (namely, Kurt Goldstein) and the non-behavioristic psychology of comportment (see *In den Netzen der Lebenswelt*, 1985, 132–33; *Antwortregister*, 1994, 457–61). An equivalent to responsivity can be found in Mikhail Bakhtin who, in his theory of the novel, uses the unusual expression *otvetnost* (Bakhtin 1979, 233), which is rendered in English as "answerability." Finally, there is a special proximity in French between responding and taking responsibility in the expression *répondre de . . .* , which means that one takes responsibility for something or somebody. Levinas and also Blanchot pursue this connection. I refer to chapter 19 of *Deutsch-Französische Gedankengänge* under the heading "Antwort der Verantwortung," which engages Levinas and takes its motto from Blanchot: "Répondre de ce qui échappe à la responsabilité."

3. I pursued this idea for the first time in discussing open forms of follow-up in interlocutionary and interactional events (see *Ordnung im Zwielicht*, 1987, 47).

4. See "Das Paradox des Ausdrucks" in *Deutsch-Französische Gedankengänge*.

Chapter 4

1. We encounter the phrase "other minds" in Anglo-Saxon literature, namely, in the title of the 1946 article by J. L. Austin.

Chapter 6

1. Furthermore, this homogenous taxonomy no longer corresponds to the common assumption of evolutionary branching in the area of life.

2. Recent phenomenological works by Iris Därmann, Rolf Elberfeld, Birgit Grieseke, and Ichiro Yamaguchi are productive explorations of interculturality.

3. Kant determines the society which would encompass all of humankind as an "ethical-civil [*ethisch-bürgerlich*] society" which emerges in the midst of the "civil-law [*rechtsbürgerlich*] society" but, as "God's realm on earth," follows a religious heritage (*Religion Within the Boundaries of Reason Alone*, Second Division, B129–30).

4. See my *Topographie des Fremden* (1997), chapter 4: "Phänomenologie als Xenologie," as well as the article "Xenologie: Wissenschaft vom Fremden" in *Historisches Wörterbuch der Philosophie*, vol. 12. See also the recent monograph by Iris Därmann: *Fremde Monde der Vernunft* (2005), which examines in detail the provocation of philosophy by ethnology.

5. Borrowing from Aristotle who, in his *Rhetoric* (3.2–3), determines the alien as a divergence (ἐξαλλάττειν, literally: a "making different") from the common use of language.

References

Aristotle. 1984. *Metaphysics*. In *The Complete Works of Aristotle I–II*, ed. J. Barnes. Princeton: Princeton University Press.

Bakhtin, M. 1979. *Die Ästhetik des Wortes*. Frankfurt am Main: Suhrkamp.

Bedorf, T. 2003. *Dimensionen des Dritten: Sozialphilosophische Modelle zwischen Ethischem und Politischem*. Munich: Fink.

Borsò, V. 1994. *Mexiko jenseits der Einsamkeit—Versuch einer interkulturellen Analyse*. Frankfurt am Main: Suhrkamp.

Bühler, K. 1982. *Sprachtheorie*. Stuttgart and New York: UTB.

Calvino, I. 1983. *Palomar*. Turin: Einaudi.

———. 1988. *Lezioni Americane*. Mailand: Garzanti.

Crary, J. 1999. *Suspensions of Perception: Attention, Spectacle and Modern Culture*. Cambridge, Mass.: MIT Press.

Dabag, M., A. Kapust, and B. Waldenfels, eds. 2000. *Gewalt, Strukturen, Formen, Repräsentationen*. Munich: Fink.

Därmann, I. 2005. *Fremde Monde der Vernunft: Die ethnologische Provokation der Philosophie*. Munich: Fink.

Elias, N. 1987. *Die Gesellschaft der Individuen*. Frankfurt am Main: Suhrkamp.

Habermas, J. 1996. *Einbeziehung des Anderen*. Frankfurt am Main: Suhrkamp.

Husserl, E. 1950– . *Husserliana* (= *Hua*). The Hague and Dordrecht: Kluwer.

———. 1950. *Cartesianische Meditationen und Pariser Vorträge* (= *Hua* I). The Hague: M. Nijhoff. English translation: *Cartesian Meditations*, trans. D. Cairns. Dordrecht: Kluwer, 1965.

———. 1954. *Die Krisis der europäischen Wissemchaften und die transzendentale Phänomenologie* (= *Hua* VI). The Hague: M. Nijhoff. English translation: *The Crisis of European Sciences and Transcendental Phenomenology*. Northwestern University Press, Evanston, 1970 (= *Crisis*).

———. 1966. *Analysen zur passiven Synthesis* (= *Hua* XI). The Hague: M. Nijhoff. English translation: *Analyses Concerning Passive and Active Synthesis*, trans. Anthony J. Steinbock. Dordrecht: Kluwer, 2001 (= *ACPAS*).

———. 1976. *Ideen zu einer reinen Phänomenologie und phänomenologischen Philosophie*. Erstes Buch: Allgemeine Einführung in die reine Phänomenologie. (= *Hua* III). The Hague: M. Nijhoff. English translation: *Ideas Pertaining to a Pure Phenomenology and to a Phenomenological Philosophy, First Book. General Introduction to a Pure Phenomenology*, trans. Fred Kersten. Dordrecht: Kluwer, 1982 (= *Ideas I*).

Kafka, F. 1973. "Investigations of a Dog." In *Shorter Works,* vol. 1. Translated by M. Pasley. London: Secker & Warburg. In German as: "Forschungen eines Hundes," in *Beschreibung eines Kampfes: Novellen, Skizzen, Aphorismen aus dem Nachlaß,* in *Gesammelte Werke in 7 Bänden.* Frankfurt am Main, 1983.

Kohl, K.-H. 1993. *Ethnologie—Die Wissenschaft vom kulturell Fremden.* Munich: Beck.

Kristeva, J. 1988. *Étrangers à nous-mêmes.* Paris: Gallimard.

Laplanche, J. 1997. *Le primat de l'autre.* Paris: Flammarion.

Leroi-Gourhan, A. 1993. *Gesture and Speech.* Cambridge, Mass.: MIT Press.

Levinas, E. 1974. *Autrement qu'être ou au-delà de l'essence.* La Haye: Nijhoff. English translation: *Otherwise Than Being or Beyond Essence.* Trans. A. Lingis. Pittsburgh: Duquesne University Press, 1981.

Melville, H. 1987. *Bartleby.* New York : Chelsea House.

Merleau-Ponty, M. 1945. *Phénoménologie de la perception.* Paris: Gallimard. English translation: *Phenomenology of Perception.* Translated by C. Smith. London: Routledge, 2002.

———. 1960. "De Mauss à Lévi-Strauss." In *Signes.* Paris: Gallimard.

———. 1969. *La prose du monde.* Paris: Gallimard. English translation: *The Prose of the World.* Trans. J. O'Neill. Evanston: Northwestern University Press, 1973.

Musil, R. 1961. *The Man Without Qualities.* Translated by E. Wilkins and E. Kaiser. London: Secker & Warburg. In German as: *Der Mann ohne Eigenschaften.* Reinbek: Rowohlt, 1978.

Nietzsche, F. 1980. *Also sprach Zarathustra.* Vol. 4 of *Kritische Studienausgabe.* Berlin: De Gruyter.

———. 1984. *Kritische Studienausgabe* (= *KSA*). Edited by G. Colli and M. Montinari. Munich: Dtv.

Rohde-Dachser, C., and F. Wellendorf, eds. 2004. *Inszenierungen des Unmöglichen: Theorien und Therapie schwerer Persönlichkeitsstörungen.* Stuttgart: Klett-Cotta.

Sterne, L. 1950. *The Life and Opinions of Tristram Shandy, Gentleman.* New York and Toronto: Modern Library.

Valéry, P. 1973. *Cahiers I.* Paris: Gallimard.

Waldenfels, B. 1980. *Der Spielraum des Verhaltens.* Frankfurt am Main: Suhrkamp.

———. 1985, 2005. *In den Netzen der Lebenswelt.* Frankfurt am Main: Suhrkamp.

———. 1990, 1998. *Der Stachel des Fremden.* Frankfurt am Main: Suhrkamp.

———. 1990. "Experience of the Alien in Husserl's Phenomenology." *Research in Phenomenology* 20 (1990): 19–33.

———. 1994. *Antwortregister.* Frankfurt am Main: Suhrkamp.

———. 1995. *Deutsch-Französische Gedankengänge.* Frankfurt am Main: Suhrkamp.

———. 1996. *Order in the Twilight.* Athens: Ohio University Press. In German as: *Ordnung im Zwielicht.* Frankfurt am Main: Suhrkamp, 1987.

———. 1997. *Topographie des Fremden.* Vol. 1 of *Studien zur Phänomenologie des Fremden.* Frankfurt am Main: Suhrkamp.

———. 1998. *Grenzen der Normalisierung.* Vol. 2 of *Studien zur Phänomenologie des Fremden.* Frankfurt am Main: Suhrkamp.

————. 1999. *Sinnesschwellen*. Vol. 3 of *Studien zur Phänomenologie des Fremden*. Frankfurt am Main: Suhrkamp.

————. 1999. *Vielstimmigkeit der Rede*. Vol. 4 of *Studien zur Phänomenologie des Fremden*. Frankfurt am Main: Suhrkamp.

————. 2000. *Das leibliche Selbst*. Edited by R. Giuliani. Frankfurt am Main: Suhrkamp.

————. 2001. *Verfremdung der Moderne*. Göttingen: Wallstein.

————. 2002. *Bruchlinien der Erfahrung: Phänomenologie, Psychoanalyse, Phänomenotechnik*. Frankfurt am Main: Suhrkamp.

————. 2004. *Phänomenologie der Aufmerksamkeit*. Frankfurt am Main: Suhrkamp.

Wittgenstein, L. 1989. "Bemerkungen über Frazer's 'Golden Bough.'" In *Vortrag über Ethik und andere kleine Schriften*, ed. J. Schulte. Frankfurt am Main: Suhrkamp.

Zahavi, D. 1999. *Self-Awareness and Alterity*. Evanston: Northwestern University Press.

Bernhard Waldenfels is a professor emeritus at the Ruhr-Universität in Bochum, where he leads a working group on phenomenology. He is the author of twenty-six books, including *Order in the Twilight* (1996), available in English.

Alexander Kozin is a research fellow in sociology at Freie Universität Berlin.

Tanja Stähler is a senior lecturer in philosophy at the University of Sussex.